#1

Pat + Carol

509 N.W Overton #3 / 3901 Northwind Drive

Portland, OR 97209   Pinson, AL 35126

11-25-89   11-25-89

She gushes like crazy!

OLD TANNEHILL

A HISTORY
OF THE
PIONEER IRONWORKS
IN
ROUPES VALLEY

(1829-1865)

By James R. Bennett

Library of Congress Catalog Card Number 86-82130
Main entry under title and subtitle:

Old Tannehill:
A History of the
Pioneer Ironworks
in Roupes Valley

Published by the Jefferson County Historical Commission in
cooperation with the Birmingham-Jefferson Historical Society
and the Tannehill Furnace & Foundry Commission, Birmingham,
Alabama.

ISBN: 0-9617257-0-2

Printed in the United States of America
1 3 5 7 9 10 8 6 4 2

ISBN 0-9617257-0-2

To Ellen who went the extra mile.

Iron seemeth a simple metal but in its nature are many mysteries. And men who bend to them their minds shall in arriving days, gather therefrom great profit, not to themselves alone but to all mankind.

Joseph Clanville
1636-1680

CONTENTS

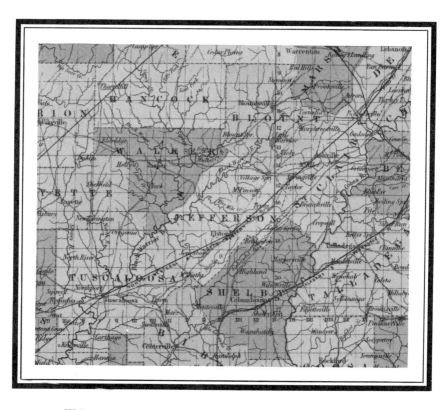

This section from Colton's Alabama map of 1853 shows the old Huntsville Road passing near the Tannehill Ironworks at McMaths along a route from Elyton to Tuscaloosa.

MAPS AND ILLUSTRATIONS

OLD TANNEHILL

The tall stone furnaces of Stroup and Sanders . . . their days of toil long past, their contribution to the Confederacy lost in time. (Alabama Department of Archives and History, Montgomery)

INTRODUCTION

To those who knew of the old ironworks ruins in the backhills of Roupes Valley near Bucksville, Old Tannehill was a special hideaway for over 100 years. With scant knowledge of the role it played in the Civil War, for visitors the tall stone furnaces of Stroup and Sanders stood alone and silent among the whispering pines, their days of toil long past, their contribution to the Confederacy lost in time.

That was before the area, rich in history as the birthplace of the Birmingham iron and steel industry, was set aside as a memorial to the old iron workers who helped make Alabama the leading industrial state in the South.

When Tannehill Historical State Park was created by the Alabama Legislature and the ironworks ordered preserved in 1969, the three Civil War period blast furnaces here were dedicated to the first generation of the industry that was to make Birmingham "the Pittsburgh of the South."

Old Tannehill, which dates from Hillman's Forge in 1830, is so rich in history that just walking its tree-shaded pathways conjures up for the visitor pictures of pioneer iron workers toiling their trade on a hot summer's day.

When it was decided a thorough history of the Tannehill Ironworks should be written, the task fell to Jim Bennett, a former newspaper reporter who was an original member of the Tannehill Furnace and Foundry Commission, the state agency the Legislature created to develop Tannehill Park. This was an opportunity he pursued with superb scholarship and dedicated vigor for a year and a half.

As a political writer for *The Birmingham Post-Herald* from 1961 to 1971, Bennett became a stalwart leader and champion in the development and operation of the new park in Roupes Valley. Twice elected to the Alabama House of Representatives, in 1978 and 1982, and to the State Senate in 1983, Bennett heralded the Tannehill development statewide.

His history covers the beginnings of the iron trade at Tannehill from Hillman's 1830 forge to Sanders' blast furnaces in 1863 and their destruction at the hands of Union cavalry in 1865. The iron-making operation at Tannehill proved that iron could be made from local ores, limestone for flux and charcoal for fuel. This made it the harbinger of the iron and steel industry in the Birmingham district which would come into full bloom only after the Civil War had ended.

vii

Also found in this work is an excellent treatise on Alabama's significant contribution to the ordnance and munitions of the Confederate Armies including tons of iron made at Tannehill for cannon and naval plate used at the Selma Arsenal.

Sen. Bennett has described the Union attack on the Tannehill Furnaces with such detail one can almost feel the heat from the Yankee torches. The author has utilized previously unpublished material in writing of the war action. This new information gives a more colorful and complete picture of what really took place on that fateful day of March 31, 1865 when units of the Eighth Iowa Cavalry put the historic iron plant out of production.

With the activities at Tannehill as background, Bennett outlines the subsequent development of the Birmingham iron and steel district that was to follow.

This work contains the most complete discussion in existence of the development of Tannehill Historical State Park which today includes some 1500 acres in Tuscaloosa, Jefferson and Bibb Counties. Reclaimed by the wilderness, Old Tannehill was dormant for almost a century. Then, in the mid-1950s interest in perserving the site as a state landmark, chiefly by individuals at the University of Alabama, began to grow. By the late 1960s the idea of a state park at the old ironworks got the blessings of the State Legislature.

Tannehill Historical State Park was born in 1969 and has been visited by thousands each year since. It's a unique and interesting place that attracted over a quarter million persons in 1984 alone reaching for a piece of Alabama history and finding it near the rushing waters of Roupes Creek.

Chriss H. Doss, Chairman
Tannehill Furnace & Foundry Commission
September 7, 1985

OLD TANNEHILL

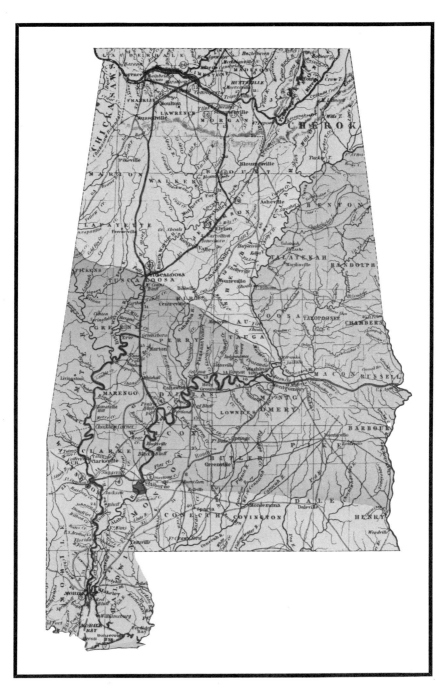

H. S. TANNER'S 1836 MAP OF ALABAMA showing stage and steamboat routes.

CHAPTER I

PATHWAYS OF DISCOVERY

"The past has contributed of its passions, its pains and its beauties; its signs you will see with us still."

— Gov. Frank M. Dixon
(Alabama, A Guide to the Deep South,
1941)

Great Appalachia, its mountain peaks dwindling into foothills, juts into northeastern Alabama like a giant dragon's tail.

Ancient and mysterious, it extends 1600 miles southward from Newfoundland before finally ending in ridges of iron ore and limestone near great beds of coal west of Birmingham.

Nowhere else in the world do all the basic ingredients of iron-making lie in such close proximity.[1]

It was this discovery that in 1846 prompted Sir Charles Lyell, an English geologist studying Southern mineral wealth, to remark Alabama's future more likely lay in the rich ore deposits of the Appalachian Plateau than the farm-rich Black Belt 100 miles to the south. He took particular note of the fact that in Roupes Valley between present day Birmingham and Tuscaloosa the essentials for ironmaking encouraged the rise of a great manufacturing center.

Lyell, president of the London Geological Society, visited the area on a trip from Mobile to Tuscaloosa, then the state capital.

"Continuing our route into the upland country," Lyell wrote, "we entered about 33 miles northeast of Tuscaloosa a region called Rook's Valley (sic Roupes) where rich beds of ironstone and limestone bid fair, from their proximity to the coal, to become one day a source of great mineral wealth."[2]

Ironically many small farmers in the area were barely getting by, unaware of the expanse of minerals sometimes just inches below their diggings. Rich planters were also more interested in cotton, corn and livestock.

The red and brown rock outcroppings, which Indians had used for war paint and for staining implements, were mere inconveniences to farming. Most early white settlers had considered the ore good only for dyeing clothes.

BIRMINGHAM was one of America's six fastest growing cities during World War I as indicated by this massive turnout for the return of the Fourth Infantry Division of the Alabama National Guard. A part of the Rainbow Division, this homecoming took place along 20th Street, May 10, 1919. (James F. Sulzby, Jr.)

So little regarded was the rocky terrain that Rev. R. K. Hargrove, a Methodist minister, passed up the chance to buy all of Red Mountain during the closing days of the Civil War — from present day Trussville to Bessemer — for $30,000.[3]

After considering the purchase Hargrove declined, not because he doubted the potential of the investment but because its development might be years in the making.

"The existence of this ore has been known to civilized men for a hundred years and they have never made any use of it, and it may be too long hence to do me or my children any good."[4]

Rev. Hargrove, who later became bishop of the Southern Methodist Episcopal Church, could not have imagined that the Birmingham area 35 years later in 1900 would rank Alabama as the nation's fourth largest producer of pig iron.[5]

Nor could he have dreamed that Birmingham, which would not be incorporated until 1871, would reach a population of 38,415 by the turn of the century, rivaling Mobile as the state's largest city. Ten years later, the 1910 Census would give Birmingham undisputed claim to the title when the population reached 132,685, more than twice the Mobile total.[6]

Bayliss Earle Grace, one of Jefferson County's pioneer settlers, was a bit more of an optimist than Hargrove. One of the first to recognize the dye rock as red ore, he sent a wagon load from his farm near the site of the Spaulding Mine south of Birmingham to the forge of Jonathan Newton Smith in Bibb County in the 1840s where it was made into wrought iron and a few blooms.[7]

Mary Gordon Duffee, who as a child in the decade before the Civil War traveled with her family from Tuscaloosa to Blount Springs, also took note of the outcroppings of iron ore along the way and pondered its future. On the trips, which followed old stage roads, she first reported seeing ore near the surface as they approached the small community of Bucksville near the Tuscaloosa and Jefferson County line. This was at the farm of Dick Murphy.

"Year in and year out, he planted and gathered his crops. In Tuscaloosa he bought his plows made of English iron to use against the rocks of iron ore in his own fields. His old face showed surprise when we asked him why he didn't reduce his ores, and the next moment he smiled as he told us he couldn't but it was a dead sure thing to be done someday. He, like the rest, had an unfaltering faith in the development of the coal and iron industry."[8]

Miss Duffee recorded her impressions in a series of 59 articles appearing in the *Birmingham Weekly Iron Age* from 1885 to 1887.

Lyell's study predicted Roupes Valley had such great mineral wealth, its future had to be influenced by it despite local agrarian interests. Even into the early 1850s, he was quoted as saying while Alabama's Black Belt region had some of the finest soil in the world, the real wealth of the state was buried in Shelby, Jefferson and Walker Counties.[9]

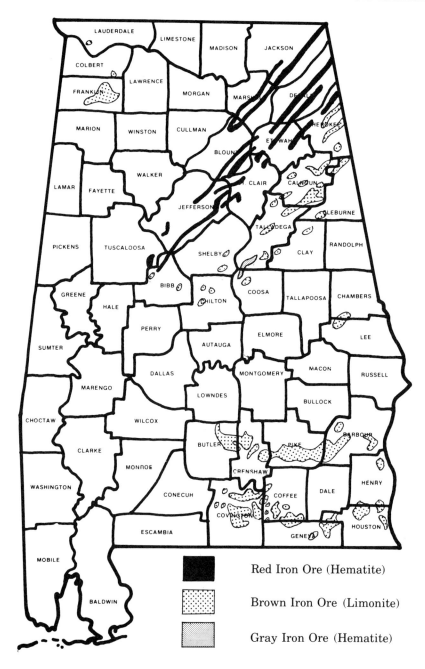

Occurrence of iron ore in Alabama (after Smith and Gilbert, 1975), Geological Survey of Alabama.

Lyell was not alone in his observations. Several of his contemporaries noted that it was one of the few areas in the world where corn and cotton grew on top of coal and iron.

John T. Maquire, a British writer visiting America in 1866, pointed to Red Mountain "as one of the elements of natural wealth out of which the brave-hearted men of Alabama would fashion a glorious future of successful industry for their country.

"It is now past refutation that steel can be made from Alabama ore as cheap as iron and that manufacturers in this state can reduce the price of steel 200 percent or more and that no state in the union can compete with Alabama in manufacturing steel by the pneumatic process."[10]

Newspapers of the day also got into the act of boasting of local mineral resources. *The Elyton Alabamian,* quoted in the *Montgomery Daily Mail,* March 19, 1858, urged:

"Come along, gentlemen and examine our iron ore, rich variegated marble, inexhaustible beds of bituminous coal and mountains of Spanish brown and lime rock . . . and you can hardly fail to be struck with the advantages afforded for turning all these minerals to immense profit. Now is the time to make good investments."

The Tuscaloosa Independent Monitor of April 16, 1859, recommended the building of a rolling mill in Alabama for the purpose of making iron rails, predicting "iron can be furnished for all the railroads that can ever be built in the state, for all time to come . . ."[11]

Systematic examination of the Roupes Valley geology began in 1848 with the appointment of Michael Tuomey as Alabama's first geologist. An Irishman who had graduated from Rensselear Polytechnic Institute, Tuomey had left a similar position in South Carolina to join the staff of the University of Alabama in 1846.

His travels on horseback, from which he mapped the state's mineral resources far more extensively than had ever been done before, frequently took him across Roupes Valley, only 33 miles northeast of Tuscaloosa.

Tuomey's survey, published in two reports, 1850 and 1858, underscored what Lyell had said about both great quantities of coal and iron ore near and in Red Mountain and Roupes Valley.

Red Mountain, Tuomey said, is an "exceedingly persistent part of the Clinton formation" which extends from New York through Appalachia into northern Alabama. Its red ore, 50 feet thick in some places, he noted, could be easily mined.

His maps and data on Alabama's mineral resources became a guide book for all sorts of pioneer ironmasters who, with the help of the Confederate government beginning in 1861, began to locate blast furnaces, rolling mills and factories close to essential deposits.

Their efforts made Alabama the "Arsenal of the Confederacy," a development which would have far-reaching influence on the direction local industry would take into the next century.[12]

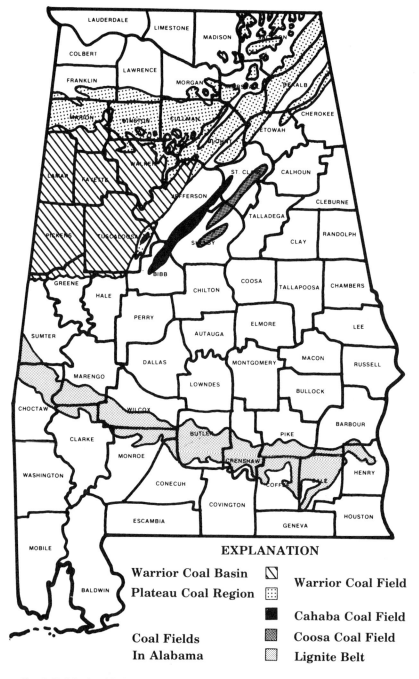

Warrior Coal Basin ◻   Warrior Coal Field

Plateau Coal Region ⠿   Cahaba Coal Field

                        Coosa Coal Field

Coal Fields
In Alabama   Lignite Belt

Coal fields in Alabama, Geological Survey of Alabama, 1985

In Roupes Valley alone, Tuomey reported, the brown hemitite ore bed near Bucksville in the vicinity of the Tannehill Ironworks "is about 100 feet thick and runs some 28 miles along a path where there is scarcely a half mile where iron ore may not be found."[13]

Tuomey also documented coal outcroppings all the way from Mount Sano near Huntsville to Roupes Valley below present day Bessemer. That there was coal in Alabama and plenty of it had been known to geologists in even earlier periods. T. A. Conrad referred to a "spot near Tuscaloosa" as a locality of bituminous coal in "Fossil Shells of the Tertiary Formations of North America" in 1832.

Coal was being mined in Tuscaloosa County near the University of Alabama as early as 1831 where it sold for four cents a bushel. It was also shipped down the river to Mobile that year, one of the earliest dates recorded for a coal operation in Alabama.[14]

Professor R. T. Brumby, in "Barnard's Almanak" of 1838, described the Warrior Coal Field as being "no less than 90 miles long from northeast to southwest with a breadth of from 10 to 30 miles extending through the counties of Tuscaloosa, Walker, Jefferson and Blount, on both sides of the Warrior River . . ."[15]

Lyell, writing in his "Second Visit to the United States of America" in 1849, also speaks of the Warrior Coal Field. The English geologist said the Warrior Field was pointed out to him by Robert Kennon, then pastor of the First United Methodist Church of Tuscaloosa. Outcroppings could clearly be seen on the banks of the Black Warrior River not far from an old covered bridge that connected Northport to Tuscaloosa.

As far as early commerce went, the Warrior Field was far more important than Alabama's other two known fields of the day, the Coosa and the Cahawba.

Coal from the Warrior during the 1850s could be purchased in Tuscaloosa for 10 to 12 cents per bushel. Coal from the Coosa Field, shipped downstream to Montgomery, sold for 40 cents per bushel.[16]

At the outbreak of hostilities between the North and South in 1861, most Alabama iron producers, however, still relied on charcoal, with coal and coke being used only in experiments.

The late J. Frank Glazner, professor of geography at Jacksonville State University from 1921 to 1952, called the Appalachian region — and its attendant mineral resources — one of the most remarkable physiographic provinces of the eastern United States.

That area of Alabama, he contended in a paper written for *The Southern Magazine* in 1934, has largely been overlooked by history although it could rightfully be called the "Ruhr Valley of the Confederacy." Here were located not only the chief iron ore deposits of the South but, during the Civil War, 20 blast furnaces, five rolling mills and numerous bloomeries and forges.[17] If Virginia's Shenandoah Valley could be called the "Granary of the Confederacy" for its food production, he said, Alabama's Great Appalachian Valley was equally noteworthy for its iron manufacture.

Even before the war period, seven and possibly eight stone blast furnaces were built in Alabama. Among the more historic of these was Old Tannehill which Ethel Armes, who wrote an exhaustive study of the state's iron and coal industry in 1910, described as being "the most haunting" of all early Alabama furnaces.

Also known as Roupes Valley Ironworks and even later as Sanders Ironworks, the old ironmaker has beginnings traceable to 1829-30 as a forge on the banks of Roupes Creek.

The operation, although small by modern standards, may well have marked the beginning of the Birmingham iron and steel industry. Although Tannehill lies just outside the Jefferson County line near Bucksville, history reveals an interesting footnote regarding the Birmingham area which now leads the entire state in iron production. Until 1861, of the 27 iron establishments — furnaces, forges and bloomeries — excluding blacksmith shops, which existed in Alabama, not one was located in Jefferson County. Early records mention only one small blacksmith shop in Elyton, now a part of Birmingham.[18]

CIVIL WAR COAL CAR, one of several discovered in 1978 when U.S. Steel was constructing a new mine near Gurnee in Shelby County. Undisturbed for 113 years, the car and a span of wooden track made of chestnut, are now on display at the Iron and Steel Museum of Alabama at Tannehill Historical State Park. (Joe Aloia)

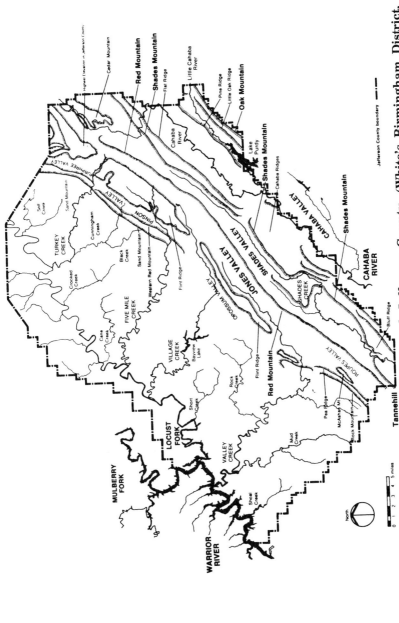

TOPOGRAPHIC FEATURES of Roupes Valley and Jefferson County. (White's Birmingham District, An Industrial History and Guide, 1981)

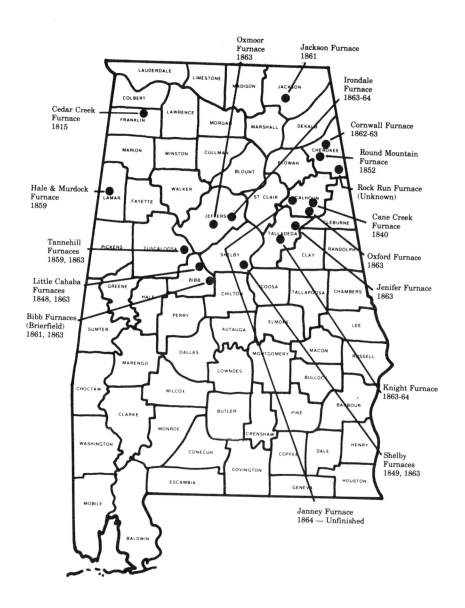

SITE LOCATIONS

Alabama Iron Furnaces Before 1865; Dates of Origin

CHAPTER II

AN IRON LEGACY HAS SHAKY BEGINNINGS

"The existence of bituminous coal in Alabama, joined to the possession of an abundant supply of good ores, at once gave Alabama prominence as a state which would before many years boast a large iron industry, and this promise is now being fulfilled."

— James Moore Swank
(The Manufacture of Iron in All Ages, 1892)

While developments at Tannehill would have definite influence on the future of the iron and steel industry in the Birmingham district, iron manufacture in Alabama actually got its start four years before the state was carved from the Mississippi Territory.

Alabama's earliest ironworks — put into blast about 1815 — was the Cedar Creek Furnace located a few miles west of Russellville in Franklin County. Its construction coincided with Napoleon's defeat at Waterloo. The brainchild of a young Pennsylvania ironmaster, Joseph Heslip, it followed stepped-up interest in Southern iron development on the heels of the War of 1812.

While the exact date that Heslip blew in his furnace is not known, one of his children was born at the Cedar Creek Ironworks in 1815, and this information was recorded in the family Bible.[19]

It was not until 1818 that Heslip, however, bought clear title to his lands from the government for $2 an acre, giving rise to conjecture on the part of some historians that Cedar Creek was not built until that year. Its contruction was of the old Roman style, a truncated pyramid of hand-hewn stone lined with brick made of local clay. It is safe to assume from evidence of other early Alabama furnaces that much of the work, including the brick draft stack, was performed by slave labor.

In 1819, when Alabama was admitted to the Union, the total population of the state was only 128,000, about half of which was slave.[20]

Brown limonite ore of the Lafayette Formation was found at the site, mined on the surface and hauled to the plant by wagon. The surrounding wilderness supplied an abundance of wood for charcoal which, made in pits, was used for fuel.

ALABAMA'S FIRST BLAST FURNACE — The Cedar Creek Furnace, built by Joseph Heslip near Russellville in Franklin County in 1815, from mural by Conrad Albrizio (1938) at Russellville Post Office. (Roger Bedford)

TANNEHILL NO. 1, built by Moses Stroup in 1859. Birthplace of the Birmingham iron industry, Tannehill Historical State Park. (George Flemming)

Faced with problems of transportation and later a cholera outbreak, Cedar Creek — also known as the Alabama Ironworks and Old Napier — left a legacy of hard times mixed with flourishes of success for ironmakers to come.

Abandoned about 1827, this earliest adventure into Alabama ironmaking seems to have had a disquieting effect on other plans to build furnaces in the state.

Alabama's second furnace, Cane Creek near Anniston in Calhoun County, did not go into blast until 1840 or 1843. The furnace was the work of Jacob Stroup, another in a long line of Pennsylvania ironmasters who would make Alabama home.

Stroup is also credited with having built the first ironworks in Georgia and South Carolina.[21] His eldest son, Moses, would go on to gain fame in his own right as builder of three Alabama furnaces, Round Mountain (1852), Tannehill No. 1 (1859) and Oxmoor (1863).

Between 1840 and the start of hostilities during the Civil War in 1861, seven furnaces would be built in Alabama in a slow but methodical industrial expansion begun at Cane Creek.

All these furnaces were similar in that they followed the same basic design, a truncated pyramid built of stone blocks around a hollow chamber, the height ranging from 19 to 40 feet and in the bosh (the widest portion of the chamber) from four to eight feet in diameter. A brick draft stack might extend another 10 to 20 feet.

The work almost always involved slave labor, although the proprietor or ironmaster may not have actually been a slave owner. It was a common practice of the day to hire slaves from local owners on an annual basis. The operator would feed, clothe and guard the slaves.

Some slaves, no doubt, became accomplished artisans at both furnace construction and operation and their value increased accordingly. The skill they possessed is evidenced today by the fine quality of workmanship and structural stability in Alabama's four or five surviving antebellum furnaces.

The best examples of this may be seen at Tannehill Historical State Park near Bessemer, Brierfield Ironworks Park near Montevallo, Cornwall Furnace near Gaylesville and Janney Furnace near Ohatchee.

Early Alabama ironworks were largely rural operations located near ore beds, a stream for water power and alongside large stands of timber needed for charcoal. They were all located near a hillside used to anchor the charging bridge as they were top-fed a mixture of ore, limestone and charcoal.

In many cases the blowing equipment consisted of one or more barrel-like cylinders activated by a water wheel, the blast pressure of which seldom exceeded two to three pounds. Other furnaces utilized huge bellows, the kind used by blacksmiths but larger. In later years, steam engines would be added as an innovation to improve production. Steam-powered blowers enabled ironmasters to continue work even in times of flood or drought.

LITTLE CAHABA FURNACE

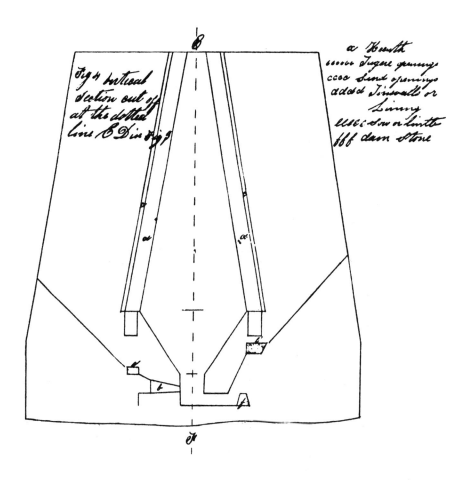

Original plan of first Little Cahaba Furnace, drawn about 1846. This is the oldest Alabama blast furnace plan known to exist. (Alabama Blast Furnaces, Woodward Iron Company)

A furnace 30 feet high and six feet in diameter was capable of producing three to eight tons of pig iron per day, depending upon the quality of the ore. Molten iron was tapped into small sand beds, called pigs, at the furnace bottom. Hollowware, at times, was cast directly into molds. Many of these furnaces also had small forges where iron was reheated and beaten into plow points, fire dogs and other implements. Some even had foundries where iron was cast into kettles and machine parts as was the case at Tannehill.

Interestingly enough, Alabama had no "mansion furnaces" like Virginia where a small ironworks would be a part of a plantation. In Alabama, iron furnaces were free-standing industries. Because of their location, bar iron from such operations was usually carried by ox cart over weathered country roads to either railheads or river ports, often 25 miles or more distant.

Most of the pig iron produced by pioneer Alabama ironmakers was shipped to foundries or machinery manufacturers. The remainder was sold or bartered to farmers, blacksmiths or small store operators in the immediate area.

With the advent of the Civil War, however, most of Alabama's iron began finding its way into Confederate arsenals, either at Selma or Rome, Georgia for military uses.

Following the construction of Cane Creek in 1840 — which plant recorded the first iron industry fatality in Alabama when a rock fall killed one of the slaves working in the ore pits[22] — came two other furnaces in rapid succession, Little Cahaba in Bibb County (1848) and Shelby Furnace in Shelby County (1849).

All three ironworks added interesting historical footnotes. In 1847 Cane Creek was supplying iron for the new state capitol in Montgomery and for the military in the Mexican War. Rebuilt in 1857, Cane Creek iron was much in demand in the Civil War when it was rolled into iron plate for the Merrimack.[23] The ironclad was subsequently renamed the "Virginia" by the Confederates.

Working drawings for Little Cahaba (also called Brighthope) are the oldest known to exist for any Alabama furnace. A second and larger furnace (Little Cahaba No. 2) was added in 1863 under contract with the Confederate government.

Shelby went into blast in 1848 about the same time as the Great California Gold Rush. The first hot blast equipment in Alabama was installed here in 1855 by Horace Ware when the plant was modernized.[24] In 1858 a rolling mill was added and a second furnace (Shelby No. 2), larger and made of brick, was built in 1863 to aid the Confederate war effort.

In the spring of 1864 plant operators here successfully used bituminous coal in the raw state for the first time in Alabama as a replacement for charcoal. Although the experiment was a success, the practice was not widely followed by other ironworks because of the non-availability of coal near furnace sites.[25]

THE MERRIMACK, renamed the Virginia by the Confederates after its conversion into an ironclad, contained iron from Alabama's Cane Creek Furnace. (Drawn from Harper's Weekly. Alabama Department of Archives and History, Montgomery)

THE CSS TENNESSEE, withstood massive federal fire in the Battle of Mobile Bay. Part of her armor plate was rolled at Alabama's Shelby Ironworks. (From photograph presented to Capt. George H. Perkins of Chickasaw, Alabama Department of Archives and History, Montgomery)

Part of the iron used as armor plate on the CSS Tennessee was rolled at Shelby. The quality of the iron may be judged from the fact the "Tennessee" successfully withstood the firepower of 17 federal vessels during the Battle of Mobile Bay without a single shell penetrating her armor.[26]

With the capacity of its two furnaces, 23 to 28 tons per day, Shelby probably provided more iron to the Selma Arsenal than any other Alabama ironworks although the exact tonnage is not known.

Three more furnaces were put into blast in the state prior to the start of the Civil War, Round Mountain in Cherokee County (1852), the first ironworks to use red fossilferrous ore from the Clinton Formation,[27] Hale and Murdock Furnace in Lamar County (1859), the first and only ironworks built in western Alabama, and Tannehill No. 1 (1859) in Tuscaloosa County, whose rich history may have sparked the present day Birmingham steel district.

Moses Stroup, who would later figure prominently into building of Oxmoor Furnace in Jefferson County (1863), built both the Round Mountain Ironworks and Tannehill No. 1.

Hale and Murdock was the only Alabama furnace to escape destruction by Union forces during the Civil War. Because of its remote location, it continued to operate until four years after the war, finally going out of blast in January of 1870 largely because of transportation problems.[28]

During the war years a dozen or more new furnaces were put into blast, Bibb No. 1 in Bibb County (1861), Cornwall Furnace in Cherokee County (1862-63), Shelby No. 2, Oxford Furnace in Calhoun County, Little Cahaba No. 2, Oxmoor, Jenifer Furnace in Talladega County, Tannehill Nos. 2 and 3 in 1863 and Irondale Furnace in Jefferson County and Knight Furnace in Talladega County, both in 1864.

Armes, in the *Story of Coal and Iron in Alabama,* lists two more, Rock Run in Cherokee County and Jackson Furnace in Jackson County, which are not mentioned in Woodward's *Alabama Blast Furnaces.*

Little is known about these works although the Jackson Furnace apparently was built around 1861 in an area that also produced coal and saltpeter for the Confederacy.[29] Rock Run Furnace fell victim to Streight's Raid early in the war. A larger post-war blast furnace was built here in 1873 but no mention is made in Woodward's research about an earlier operation ever existing here.

One of the more speculative furnace operations in war-time Alabama was the ill-fated Janney Furnace near Ohatchee in Calhoun County which was hit by Union forces under Gen. Lovell H. Rousseau July 14, 1864 before it could ever be put into blast.

A. A. Janney, a foundryman from Montgomery who had used iron extensively from the Cane Creek Furnace only five miles away, began the new works late in 1863 still optimistic the South could win the war. It apparently was ready to begin making iron about the time Union forces arrived.

CORNWALL FURNACE, built by the Noble Brothers near Gaylesville in Cherokee County late in 1862 or early 1863. Its high main arch distinguished it from other Civil War period Alabama ironmakers. (Birmingham Public Library)

BIBB NO. 2, also known as Bibb Naval Furnace or Brierfield, built by Confederate Government in 1863. The large brick furnace provided a good portion of the iron used for ironclads and large naval ordnance. (Birmingham Public Library).

The Bibb Furnace, also known as Brierfield and later Strother, followed by 13 years the first ironworks to be built in Bibb County, the Little Cahaba (1848).

At first the iron produced here was for local agricultural and domestic purposes but as the need for Confederate war materials grew, the government sought to buy the plant's entire output. When the operators — who eyed a lucrative market with iron-short planters — declined, a "forced sale" was ordered in the amount of $600,000 in Confederate money.[30]

In 1863 the Confederacy began construction of Bibb No. 2, a large brick furnace equipped with hot blast. It would become known as the Bibb Naval Furnace. The ironworks, now completely in government hands along with a nearby rolling mill, sent its entire output to the Selma Arsenal, some of which was used in plates for Confederate gunboats. Woodward, however, says most of the iron was cast into large naval ordnance for which it became famous.

Because it was a government-owned operation, the Bibb Furnaces did not experience the shortage of skilled and non-skilled labor which beset many of its sister furnaces around the state. After the war, the property — laid in ruin by Union forces — was confiscated by the federal government as contraband of war and in 1866 was put up for public sale.

Cornwall, like Bibb, had a direct government influence. The Noble Brothers Foundry at Rome, Georgia ranked second to Selma as a Deep South Confederate supplier of large field ordnance.

There was not, however, a sufficient supply of pig iron and as a consequence, the Nobles, with financial help from the Confederacy, began construction of Cornwall Furnace in Cherokee County in 1862.

Because it was built a short distance from the Chattooga River, it was necessary to dig a canal about a half mile long. Woodward says the ore used here was red hematite from Dirtseller Mountain three miles distant. Almost all the iron produced at this site went to Rome.

Oxford Furnace, the second ironmaker built in Calhoun County (Janney was the third), went into blast in April of 1863, like others before it to bolster the Confederacy's iron supply.

There was a direct connection between this plant and the first blast furnace in the South to manufacture coke iron (1860). When the East Tennessee Iron Company in Chattanooga went out of business, a portion of its machinery was sent to Oxford.

Tuomey, as early as 1848-49, made note of the great potential for the iron trade in Calhoun County (then called Benton), particularly in the Anniston area.

> "The vicinity of a bold stream, abundance of fuel, excellent building material and proximity to a railroad, point to this locality as the site of one of the future great iron manufacturing establishments of the state."[31]

JANNEY FURNACE, construction of which began by A. A. Janney near Ohatchee in Calhoun County late in 1863, was destroyed by federal troops before it could be put into blast, July 14, 1864. One of the most pretentious of Alabama's Civil War period ironworks, it can be seen today near Anniston, off County Road 62. (Alabama Blast Furnaces, Woodward)

Tuomey's prediction would come true in 1873 when the Woodstock Iron and Steel Company put into blast on the site of the old Oxford Ironworks the first of four large Anniston furnaces that would make the North Alabama city a leader in iron production.

During the Civil War period Jefferson County got its first official taste of ironmaking beginning with Oxmoor in November of 1863 followed by Irondale in December of the same year. Both would have far reaching influence on building Birmingham as the South's leading iron producer at the turn of the century.[32]

Oxmoor, the construction of which was supervised by Moses Stroup, was a copy of the older furnace at Tannehill which he had built between 1855 and 1859. Located in Shades Valley between the present day communities of Homewood and Shannon, Oxmoor used Red Mountain iron ore from diggings a short distance away. Oxmoor iron was shipped to Selma and Rome on the Selma, Rome and Dalton Railroad.

The furnace at Irondale, also known as the Cahawba or McElwain Ironworks, was built in upper Shades Valley and like Oxmoor, on the banks of Shades Creek. The two furnaces were only 10 miles apart.

Some time during the spring or early summer of 1864 the first successful coke iron made in Alabama was produced at Irondale.[33] Somewhat larger than Oxmoor, Irondale Furnace featured a stack of heavy masonry at the base and was of brick, banded with iron ties, on the mantle.

Both laid in ruin by Wilson's Raiders in March of 1865, Irondale was rebuilt and operated until 1873. Oxmoor, also rebuilt and enlarged, remained active until 1927, an ironmaking period that would span 64 years.[34]

In 1876 after the Oxmoor Furnaces had been rebuilt (Oxmoor No. 2 was added in 1873), coke iron was produced here using a more modern technology, thus assuring the future growth of the coal and iron industry in the Birmingham area.

As in Jefferson, two furnaces were also built in Talladega County during the war years, the first being Jenifer near Munford in 1863. It was followed by the Knight Furnace some three and a quarter miles away in early 1864.

Despite its early beginnings, the iron industry had been slow to expand in Alabama until the advent of the Civil War increased need for iron and military equipment.

The Census of Manufacturers of 1860, for instance, indicates that the industrial development of the nine southeastern states lagged behind the rest of the country. The area had 22% of the population compared to 6.5% of the capital invested in manufacturing enterprises, 5.4% of the workers employed and 5.2% of the value of its products.[35]

IRONDALE FURNACE, as it appeared about 1893. Built by W. S. McElwain in 1863 as Jefferson County's second ironworks. Its remains can still be seen today off Stone River Road in Mountain Brook. (Alabama Department of Archives and History, Montgomery)

Of the 15 iron producing plants in operation in Alabama during the Civil War, Armes says none were more historically-rooted than Old Tannehill located near the junction of four Alabama counties, Tuscaloosa, Jefferson, Bibb and Shelby.

With beginnings traceable to 1829, Tannehill's three cold blast furnaces made it the only site in Alabama during the Civil War where as many furnaces operated side by side.

COL. TANNEHILL'S old house, on the Bucksville Road about 1910, is now just a memory. (Armes)

EAGLE FORGE on Talladega Creek, Talladega County (1846). Built by George D. Wheeler and Israel Sprayberry, it may have been similar in design to Daniel Hillman's first forge at Tannehill in 1830. (Iron and Steel Museum of Alabama)

ROUPES CREEK which runs in front of the old Tannehill Ironworks is as scenic as it is historic. Here early furnace workers rested on a hot summer's day.

CHAPTER III

OLD TANNEHILL

"Solemnly the old furnace speaks of the heavy ways of toil, long since dead, that our fathers had before us. Majestic in the forest, yet ruling no more, it has a burdened, solitary heart . . . The very shadows seem to sleep, even as the stones; and the drowsy sun rays circling them are but the brushing wings of evanescent dreams."

— Ethel Armes
(The Story of Coal and Iron in Alabama, 1910)

In 1830, shortly after Andrew Jackson assumed the presidency, Daniel Hillman, an old furnaceman from New Jersey, built a forge on the banks of Roupes Creek hoping to find his fortune in Alabama's infant iron trade.

Until the erection of Hillman's Forge, which he promptly dubbed the Roupes Valley Ironworks, Blount, Jefferson and Walker Counties had only meager iron supply and the potential for a good market was obvious.

The land on which the little ironmaker was built had been granted to Col. Ralph McGehee of Montgomery by the United States in 1829. McGehee and several other planters decided to invest in Roupes Valley and found in Hillman the expertise needed for success.

In reference to the early forge, Baylis E. Grace, whose accounts in the *Jefferson Record* and other publications would become valuable benchmarks in the development of the iron industry in central Alabama, wrote in the mid-1800s:

"Several planters with means, among them Ralph McGehee and Richard B. Walker, settled on the north side of the Cahaba River. Impressed with the immense deposits of brown hematite ore in Roupes Valley, they decided to try the experiment of making iron on a cheap scale for the Jefferson County settlers, the nearest market for bar iron being Tuskaloosa. The company got Hillman of New Jersey and erected a little furnace on a bold stream which runs across Roupes Valley and flows into Shades Creek. Here a large hammer propelled by water hammered out the best kind of tough metal and supplied the counties for some distance around with plows, horseshoes and hollow ware."[36]

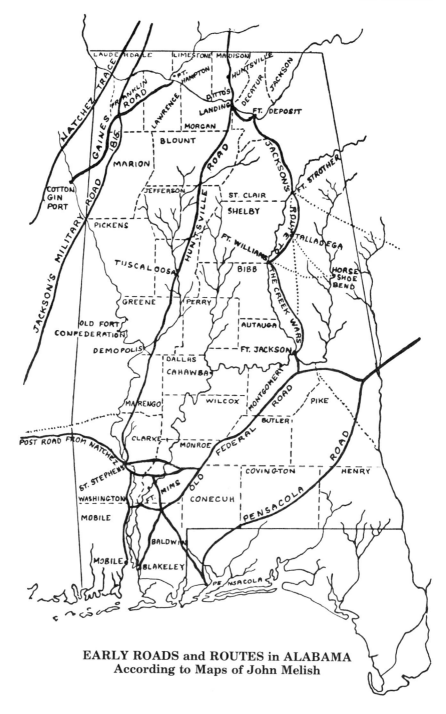

EARLY ROADS and ROUTES in ALABAMA
According to Maps of John Melish

From such beginnings was born the Birmingham district's first formal iron operation. Although the location of the ironworks was in Tuscaloosa County, the forge was purposely located near a point where four counties — Tuscaloosa, Jefferson, Bibb and Shelby — came together in order to command a good market. Years later the State Legislature moved the Shelby County line some five miles to the east.

Hillman's pioneer forge, fired by charcoal made from wood cut in the immediate area along with brown ore from nearby pockets, produced iron which sold for 10 cents a pound. By comparison, sugar in 1830 cost 15 cents a pound and coffee, 40 cents.[37]

Prior to this operation numerous efforts were reportedly made by local blacksmiths to utilize the ore, mixing lime rock, but their products were too brittle to allow reheating or hammering into shape on the anvil. The McGehee-Hillman effort was the first successful attempt to make iron in Roupes Valley and would point the way for other such ventures to follow in the Birmingham area.

Baylis Grace, who visited Hillman's Forge, said farmers had their plows made of his iron and the horses shod with it, a good test he reasoned for making car wheels for the industry one day.

Grace, who would serve a term as Jefferson County sheriff, was among the first to recognize the promise of Alabama iron ore, having sold the first shipment of it for manufacturing purposes to Oxmoor Furnace, and later became an agent for the Thomas Iron Company of Pennsylvania, a predecessor of Republic Steel Corporation.

With no railroads in the area, Hillman was forced to haul his product by ox cart some 35 miles distant to Tuscaloosa, then the state capital, over rough country roads that were all but impassable in bad weather. Coupled with the problems of finding skilled labor, his success won for him the distinction of being called "the founder of the iron trade in Alabama."[38] To him also belongs the honor of making the first wrought iron in the state.[39]

Miss Duffee, who chronicled Alabama's early iron industry in newspaper columns in the late 1880s during a period of sharp industrial growth in Birmingham, gave to Hillman the credit of launching the manufacture of iron in the area.

"After a very careful comparison of notes, I am led to believe that the first iron ever made in the present wonderland of the South was at a locality on Roupes Creek, some two miles east of the well-known McMath place, and near the corners of four counties, vis: Tuscaloosa, Jefferson, Shelby and Bibb."[40]

Although McGehee furnished the financing, it was Hillman's genius, Miss Duffee wrote, and "unwearied skill and energy" that made the iron venture a success, "discovered the possibilities of the mineral region and demonstrated their importance and value to the demands of commerce."

Hillman, whose Dutch ancestors had been ironmasters in Europe, was born in Philadelphia, Pennsylvania where his father had instructed him in wagon making and blacksmithing.

After the family suffered from several economic setbacks, Daniel Hillman and his brother, James, moved to New Jersey where he put enough capital together in 1814 to set up a small plant near Valley Forge.

Here he married, purchased a farm and a store and several wagons. Before his ironworks had cleared the debts owed against it, Ames says, a flood washed it away and his partner skipped town forcing him to sell his possessions and move on.

Hillman, in search of new iron territory, then moved to Ohio where he built a forge on the banks of Paint Creek near Chillicothe in 1819, then the state capital. This operation is one of the earliest on record in Ohio.

Several years later after his wife and five children had joined him, Hillman moved again, this time to Kentucky where he set up still another forge in Bath County. With help from his four sons, Daniel Jr., James, George and Charles, he put together an even more ambitious ironworks at Greenup, Kentucky in 1823 where he made flatboats and engaged in shipping iron and coal to markets in Cincinnati. All four boys would go on to make names for themselves in the iron trade in Kentucky, Tennessee and Alabama.

Hillman's only daughter, Jane Hillman, married Justus Buck Goodrich whose son, Levin S. Goodrich, helped make the first pig iron from coke at Oxmoor in 1876. When Hillman's wife died, the old ironmaker returned to Ohio for a short while where he managed the Pine Grove Steam Furnace at Hanging Rock. Still restless he soon thereafter accompanied several members of the Goodrich family to New Orleans where they were to make a shipment of iron to Mobile.

It was in Mobile where Hillman, still following the scent of iron, heard of deposits in Roupes Valley which would turn out to be the richest pockets of brown ore he had ever seen.

A letter written from this location to his son, George, dated August 21, 1830, is as follows:

"Dear Son: These lines will inform you that I am well, and I hope that you and your brothers, sister and son, are the same. I shall start one forge for Colonel McGehee in about four or five weeks, and then expect to build a sawmill for myself. I can sell about $2,000 worth of plank. I can cut pine timber on Uncle Sam's land, a practice very generally prevailing in this country. Colonel McGehee will assist me in any way, so I can get him a-going in a short time. He will want material for his furnace which he will commence building about Christmas. I am to superintend the building of it, and immediately afterwards the building of another forge unless something prevents.

"I believe, George, that my prospects for making a handsome property are better than they ever were during all the course of my life. I wrote to Daniel and desired him to come to this country; for there is one of the best prospects I ever saw for him to make a fortune. I shall write to him and give particulars of the prospects. It is as healthy here as in any part of Kentucky.

DANIEL HILLMAN, JR.
(Armes)

T. T. HILLMAN
(UAB)

OLD HILLMAN HOSPITAL, now a part of the University of Alabama Medical Center, was named for T. T. Hillman when it opened in 1903. (University of Alabama, Birmingham)

"I have had my health I believe better, for I have gained considerably in weight since I have been here. I hope to come and see you in March, for I can go from here to Nashville in five days by stage, and then take the steamboat.

"Give my love to Daniel, Jane and Charles.

From your father,
DANIEL HILLMAN[41]

Hillman died two years later and is buried in an unmarked grave in the old cemetery at Bucksville. His sons and grandsons would later figure prominently in the development of Birmingham's iron industry. Daniel Hillman took his father's advice and came to Alabama in the late 1860s where be bought large mineral holdings in Jones Valley which would later be sold to United States Steel Corporation. His grandson, Thomas T. Hillman, was an official of the old Tennessee Coal and Iron Company. Later, with H. E. McCormack, he founded the Pratt Consolidated Coal Company. In 1879, in conjunction with Colonel Henry F. DeBardeleben, he built the Alice Furnace, the first ironworks in the city of Birmingham.

The Hillman name not only looms large in the history of ironmaking in Alabama and five other states but it is interwoven into the fabric of early day Birmingham. The old Hillman Hotel, now demolished, was named for T. T. Hillman as was Hillman Hospital, which is now a part of the University of Alabama Medical School. The community of Hillman, located between Birmingham and Bessemer, was also named for him.

The cemetery in Bucksville is the resting place for others who had a direct connection to the ironworks Daniel Hillman built. Although unincorporated, Bucksville is one of the oldest communities in Tuscaloosa County. Records reveal a post office was located in "Buck's" store in 1827. Not much remains, however, from the 19th Century there today. The oldest known building is the home of David Buck built in 1825.

Miss Duffee, who passed through the little village numerous times from 1850 to the start of the Civil War, said Bucksville was a "pretty town" with "an unromantic name."

"The buildings had a venerable air of antiquity, and a stranger was at once seized with the idea that he stood in some old deserted village."[42]

In addition to Bucksville, several other communities had sprung up in the area following the Treaty of Fort Jackson in 1814 which ended the Creek Indian War. With peace at hand, white pioneers began flooding into the state from Tennessee, Georgia and North and South Carolina.

One of the earliest of these pioneers was John Jones, who led a party of settlers into Jefferson County in 1815 and established a small community about a mile northwest of present day Bessemer, the first part of the county to be settled. Originally called Indian Mound Campground

TRACES OF THE OLD HUNTSVILLE ROAD, which date to the early
1800s, can still be seen today as it cuts across the Russell Farm near
Bucksville.

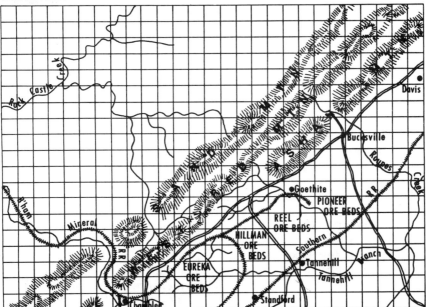

IRON ORE MINING was a major occupation of workers in the Tannehill
area both before and after the Civil War. This 1889 map of Jefferson
County clearly shows early ore beds known as Pioneer, Hillman, Reel,
Goethite and Eureka. (After E. Greig, Alabama Department of Archives
and History, Montgomery)

because of Indian mounds nearby, the town was incorporated in 1821 by act of the newly-formed State Legislature and changed its name to Jonesboro.

The little village — with its small wooden fort — became a favorite stopping point for families migrating south into and through Alabama along the old Huntsville Road. Once an Indian trail, the route cut across Jefferson County and served as a direct link between the Tennessee Valley and the emerging Black Belt. Traces of the old Huntsville Road can be seen today running almost parallel to an abandoned section of U.S. 11 just west of Bucksville.

After extinguishing Indian claims, the government sold land in this area for $2 an acre until 1820, then reduced the price to $1.25, still oblivious to the mineral riches awaiting discovery.[43]

The old Jonesboro site is located on the grounds of U.S. Steel's Dolanah dolomite quarry.

On September 17, 1819, William Roupe, a member of John Jones' original party, became the first recognized settler in the valley between Jonesboro and Tuscaloosa County. Subsequently the two valleys falling off the Appalachian Chain from Red Mountain in southwestern Jefferson County became known as Jones and Roupes Valleys. Lying partially in Jefferson and partially in Tuscaloosa County, Roupes Valley is first mentioned in official records in Acts of the Legislature, December 13, 1819, in which boundaries for Jefferson County are described.[44]

Over the next 40 years other pioneers purchased property near springs and creeks in the area and established small farms at distances of one to four miles apart. Other small communities in the area included McCalla, like Bucksville on the old Huntsville Road, and Pleasant Hill along Eastern Valley Road near the present site of McAdory School.

The brown ore that Hillman used for his Roupes Valley iron plant was part of the Goethite deposit that was mined even after the Civil War by the Pioneer Mining and Manufacturing Company and its successor, Republic Steel Corporation. Shook and Fletcher Supply Company was the last to extract ore from the area, closing out its mining operations here in 1958.

Although more modern mining techniques all but obliterated the pioneer mine sites, traces of the earliest surface mining operations can still be seen just north of the Alabama Great Southern tracks about a mile north of Tannehill Historical State Park. Hillman's ore operations were the first instance of strip mining of record in Alabama.

After Hillman's death the forge lay dormant until 1836 when it was sold to Ninian Tannehill, one of the first pioneers to settle in the valley in 1818. A cotton planter, Tannehill had moved to Alabama from South Carolina and set up a prosperous cotton business.

His marriage to Mary Prude in 1819 is the first on file in the old Elyton Courthouse in Jefferson County. The Tannehills first located in Jonesboro and near Pleasant Hill but, buying lands in Tuscaloosa County, moved there settling in Roupes Valley.[45]

NINIAN TANNEHILL
(Iron & Steel Museum)

MOSES STROUP
(Armes)

MARION TANNEHILL
(Iron & Steel Museum)

SARAH ELIZABETH
McMATH
(Iron & Steel Museum)

It was by this means that Tannehill acquired the old Hillman Forge and enlarged the operation. Although the ironworks would have other owners, it was his name which stuck. Tannehill owned some 20 slaves and, in addition to his iron operation, engaged in cotton farming and raising livestock.

The Tannehill Family, which had originated in Scotland, saw seven brothers by that name migrate to Pennsylvania during the days of its early settlement. One of the brothers, Phillip, later moved to North Carolina. His grandson, Ninian, along with four brothers, moved from South Carolina to Alabama, and they settled in different parts of the state.

Colonel Tannehill apparently considered selling his iron plant as well as his entire plantation to the Riddle Brothers of Holidaysburg, Pennsylvania in 1842.

A letter, written during a visit to the plant site July 28 of that year, by E. R. Riddle to his brother, Samuel, states he felt the Tannehill property was "well worth" the $5,000 for which it was being offered.

The Tannehill homeplace, Riddle wrote, contained about 1,000 acres, 750 of which was cleared and under fence. In addition to Tannehill's two-story frame house (see photo, page 23), the property consisted of "a gin and thrashing machine house, a grist mill running two pairs of stone, a saw mill and some other houses for hands."

Riddle continued, "On the forge site there is 240 acres, not more than 15 acres of which is cleared, some good land that might be cleared. This tract joins the house tract. On it is the forge or miserable concern that they are now running. The hammers, the wheel, shaft and forebay are new."

Riddle informed his brother that with some repairs and alterations, the plant "could be run to good advantage for some time."

While Tannehill was asking $1,800 for the forge tract, Riddle predicted it could be bought for $1,200. The forge property, he wrote, also consisted of "some good buildings for hands" and "the purest and best ore you have ever seen."

Even as early as 1842 some thought was apparently being given to enlarging the forge operation. Riddle said the tract contained "two excellent sights (sic) for furnaces or other works." A short distance below the forge, he pointed out, "there is a good situation for a forge on publick (sic) land." Rock for building a furnace here, he added, could be found in the immediate area.

The Riddles, who were railroad contractors and civil engineers in Pennsylvania, however, decided against the Tannehill offer and moved

---

Letter from E. R. Riddle to his brother, Samuel S. Riddle, is part of the private papers collection at Heritage Hall, Talladega Heritage Commission, Talladega, Alabama. Iron produced at Tannehill in 1842 was listed in the correspondence as selling for 1½¢ per pound for home market use and 7-8¢ per pound hauled to markets 50 miles away.

instead to Talladega County where they built a forge called "Maria" on Talladega Creek in 1843.

Riddle's assessment of the Tannehill property would prove prophetic. Furnaces and forges would be added at this site, although a decade or two later.

Tannehill remained on the property and continued his iron production and agricultural interests.

A letter written to Miss Armes by William W. Tannehill of Commanche, Texas (a great nephew of Col. Tannehill) states that "in August, 1849 he had his iron factory in full blast at that time and for some time before."[46]

J. B. Green was a partner of Tannehill's in the iron venture but sold out his share to him just before he died in 1843. Green was buried near his old home place not far from Woodstock in Bibb County. His grave marker, along with those of other family members, has been moved to Tannehill Historical State Park and can be seen near the old country church. Tannehill was active in a number of civic endeavors in the Bucksville area and for a time served as a justice of the peace in both Jefferson and Tuscaloosa Counties.

The Jones Valley Times lists him, along with Elisha McMath, Marion Tannehill (his son), Robert M. Huffman and Charles H. Williams as trustees of the Bucksville Male and Female High School on April 15, 1851.[47]

An advertisement for the school described the area as one "renowned for its good waters, health and moral rectitude." The school house was located a little over a mile from McMath's on the old Huntsville Road and some 24 miles from Tuscaloosa.

McMath's, the big roomy residence of Elisha McMath, was located between Bucksville and Woodstock and was known for its large spring. It was also mentioned by Tuomey as the site of brown ore outcroppings. A post office was located here in 1842. It is thought the McMath Spring is actually a part of an underground river that runs through the area and may give rise to the many springs in the vicinity.

The spring, also known as Cross Springs, is still visible just off old U.S. 11 on the Lazy D Ranch owned by the Russell interests. Until 1982 a portion of the chimney still stood but was demolished during a logging operation in the area. Two huge oaks and a large sweetgum give little hint of the grand size of the old McMath home place. In its prime, about the time McMath's daughter, Sarah, married Ninian Tannehill's son, Marion, in 1846 the McMath place was, like the nearby ironworks, an area landmark.

McMath, himself a slave owner, entertained many of Tuscaloosa County's leading citizens. It was here that Lucanda McMath, Elisha's daughter, married Joseph L. Hogg in 1832. They later moved to Texas, and their son, James Stephen Hogg, became the first native-born Texan to be elected governor of that state.[48]

GRAVE MARKERS of Ninian Tannehill, who died 1875, and J. B. Green, who died 1843, are in the furnace area. Tannehill is buried in the old cemetery in nearby Bucksville. Green's marker is near the old Country Church in Tannehill Historical State Park. They were early partners in the ironworks operation. (Joe Aloia)

Even in the days immediately after the Civil War, the McMath place apparently was falling into disrepair. Josiah Gorgas, one-time chief of ordnance for the Confederacy, visited it August 10, 1865. Of the spring, he wrote: "It is not worth looking at now, having been filled in with stones and all of its beauty destroyed."[49]

Captain H. H. Cribbs, who Armes said clerked in a store near Tannehill in 1847, recalled that the forge was operated on a regular basis and that there was a foundry in connection with it. The ore was still being mined at the old Goethite site which Hillman had opened 12 years before and transported by ox cart. Later a crude tramway was built for this purpose, more than likely using wood instead of iron rails.

Cribbs said the iron was made into ovens, skillets and kettles and shipped to Tuscaloosa, Selma and many areas throughout the Black Belt by wagon. Farmers, blacksmiths and merchants also purchased bar iron, cast iron goods and plows. An example of goods produced here, a big kettle four feet in width, can be seen at the Iron and Steel Museum of Alabama at Tannehill Historical State Park.

Located some distance from Elyton, Jonesboro or Tuscaloosa, the area around the ironworks grew into a small self-contained community complete with log houses, farms and mining operations.

The ironworks was sold to John Alexander in 1857 and it was about this time that his father-in-law, Moses Stroup, was engaged to oversee a major expansion of the plant. While some historians credit Stroup with having purchased the property and building a blast furnace on it in 1855, it is more likely that Stroup erected his new stack between 1859 and 1861 and that Alexander was the actual owner.

J. P. Lesley in the *Bulletin of the American Iron Association of 1858* lists "Stroup's Forge" as a "bloomery, making bars for home market from hematite ores, brown and fiberous (sic), from neighborhood. Made in 1857 up to October 1 . . . 60,394 pounds in 110 days."[50] That averaged out to about 27 tons. Had there been a blast furnace here in 1858, Lesley in all probability would have made mention of it.

Stroup's Forge was more than likely the same one Hillman had built with a few improvements. It is thought that Stroup began to build his cold blast charcoal furnace near the site of the "old timey" plant the next year.

Built much in the same fashion as the earlier stone furnaces in Alabama, Tannehill No. 1 used sandstone carved from a quarry site on the hillside 300 yards to the west. Many of the big stones, which were transported to the furnace site by use of skids, weighed in excess of 400 pounds. The quarry site can be seen today much the way Stroup left it a century earlier.

THE OLD ROCK QUARRY from which the heavy furnace stones were extracted is still very much in evidence a short distance from the ironworks. This photo taken around 1900. (Birmingham Public Library)

OLD DRILL HOLES mark many of the huge sandstone blocks that either fell or were discarded along the high ridge road through the quarry site. (Joe Aloia)

When the stone stack was completed, a wooden trestle was built connecting the furnace to the hillside behind it for the purpose of charging the ironworks from the top.

Machinery for the new plant was bought in Philadelphia and firebrick for the furnace's inner lining was reportedly imported from Stowbridge, England. The remains of a brick kiln, however, have been identified near the present day Tannehill Historical State Park Gift Shop, giving rise to speculation the bricks were made on site, although this operation could have been built a few years later.

Stroup's stone stack was 30 feet high and 8½ feet in the bosh. Given the obstacles of reducing the ores, it is thought production did not exceed five to six tons a day.[51]

Slave labor was used extensively in cutting the stone, building the furnace and digging charcoal pits which were located on the high ridge behind the plant. A wooden flume brought water from Roupes Creek on whose banks the furnace stood to an overshot wheel which was mounted on a wooden axle that turned on stone bearings. To the end of the axle was attached a cam which in turn operated a set of huge bellows by means of a lever. The forge hammer was also operated by water power in much the same manner.

From the hearth at the bottom of the furnace molten iron was tapped into sandbeds or ladled into molds. This operation took place in a casting shed or foundry built onto the furnace itself.

The depression in the sand where the iron poured from the "tap hole" had runners to each side resembling a sow with sucking piglets; thus came the description of "pig iron."

The craftsmanship of the furnace work — and of Furnaces Nos. 2 and 3 which would follow in 1863 — was a tribute to the skill of slave artisans whose work would stand into the next century.

Armes says the Tannehill ruins are "known far and wide as the most interesting and picturesque example of the old way of furnace building extant in the South."[52]

Slaves dug the brown hematite ore from open pits in the Goethite deposit in the same area Hillman and Tannehill received their supply some two to three miles from the plant. While there is no doubt that brown ore was used extensively in the Tannehill operation, there is a report that Stroup experimented with red ore from Red Mountain which would have been its first use on record in a blast furnace.[53]

Born in Lincoln County, North Carolina in 1794, Stroup was one of the premier ironmakers of his day. Beginning at age 11 while working with his father, he would later help put the iron industry in South Carolina and Georgia on firm footing.

"He was a remarkable genius in his way," wrote Miss Duffee. "He seemed to be endowed with a natural talent and intense personal fondness for the useful industry he so early chose as his profession, as will be shown by the fact that during his lifetime he built seven different furnaces and five rolling mills."[54]

John E. Ware, who edited *Our Daily Home* in Talladega and was the son of the builder of the Shelby Ironworks, said of Stroup: "Moses Stroup at the time of his death in 1877 was the oldest and most experienced ironmaker in the South."[55]

The Stroup family had been in the iron business since colonial times. David Stroup, Moses' grandfather, was a soldier and gunsmith for the Continental Army. He left Pennsylvania and moved to North Carolina after the Revolution and built an iron plant in Lincoln County. Moses' father, Jacob, helped in its construction at age 15.

Jacob Stroup later moved to South Carolina and put up the first ironworks in that state and helped raise a company of infantry in the War of 1812. When he sold the plant in 1827, Moses stayed and helped cast cannon for the Nullification Party. His father moved on to Georgia where he built the first iron plant there in Habersham County in 1828. In 1836, Jacob Stroup sold this operation and built still another on Stamp Creek in Cass County, Georgia. Moses joined him here again in 1843 and later bought out his father's interest.[56]

Moses' brother, Jacob Stroup Jr., in a letter to Miss Armes, wrote of the ironmaker:

> "In those days schooling was not up and Moses had none, only what he got by his pine knot light. But all his life he was a great student, well posted on every subject, and he became a man of fine judgment. He was always a good money maker, but a poor keeper. He did more in the iron industry in the South in his day and time than any other man. His knowledge of the construction and operation of blast furnaces was wonderful."[57]

After Moses Stroup took over for his father in Cass County, he enlarged the plant adding more furnaces and a rolling mill. It was here he rolled the first railroad iron in the South, strap iron used on the Old State Road which later became the Western & Atlantic.

While he was busy with the Georgia operation, his father came to Alabama and built the Cane Creek Furnace near Anniston in 1840. This was only the second ironworks built in the state.

Moses, himself, came to Alabama in 1848, two years after his father died, and began building the Round Mountain Ironworks near Centre in 1849. He had sold his Georgia interests in 1847.

The Round Mountain plant, Alabama's fifth ironworks, was put into operation in 1852 using red fossilferous ore. The furnace, which may have been a model for Tannehill No. 1, was 32 feet high and eight feet in the boshes. It employed 45 people.

Some time during 1855 Stroup sold his interest in Round Mountain to Samuel P. S. Marshall of Eddysville, Kentucky[58] and moved to Tuscaloosa County where his son-in-law, John Alexander, had purchased the forge at Tannehill from Colonel Tannehill.

Here Stroup began to modernize the plant and build tramways to existing flour and timber mills which had grown into what Armes said was a "flourishing little community."

MANY OF THE OLD FURNACE ARTIFACTS, including machinery parts, tools, pots, pipe and iron products made at Tannehill, are on display at the Iron and Steel Museum of Alabama at Tannehill Park.

When the Tannehill No. 2 (furnace) went into blast it was the first major technological rebuild in the ironmaking operation here since Hillman built his forge in 1830. In addition to his high furnace, Stroup added a foundry as well as cast houses for making plows, axes, fire dogs and all kinds of hollowware.

"The great difficulty in getting men of capital to come here from the North," Stroup wrote in 1859, "is you cannot get them to believe what we say about this country and they won't believe it is healthy here."[59]

Undoubtedly, much of the iron produced during this period was sold or bartered around the countryside to planters and storekeepers. Vegetables and clothing were as important as money because the slaves, hired from their owners, had to be fed and clothed.

In the vicinity of the ironworks Stroup located a store or commissary, a nail factory, various small forges and nearby dozens of slave houses. Most of these were thought to be located on an old charcoal haul road coming off Eastern Valley Road on the northeast side of Tannehill Mill Creek (also known as Cooley Creek). The trail is the same one which runs from Hall's Mill at Tannehill Historical State Park across Farley Field toward the base of a high cliff where it fords the stream and enters the furnace yard.

Foundation stones of structures thought to have been housing for several hundred slaves who worked in the Tannehill operation during the war period have been located along the old roadway as well as those of a large blacksmith shop and a building which may have housed government workers or Confederate soldiers. A slave cemetery has also been located about a half mile to the east over the high ridge trail or iron haul road to Montevallo. The old road was designated a National Boy Scout Hiking Trail in 1973.

There are reports that as many as 600 slaves worked at Tannehill at one time in all phases of the operation including iron manufacture, timber cutting, charcoal production, ore mining and transportation.

Armes says something like 3,400 acres of heavy timber were cut for charcoal during the lifetime of the old furnaces. Manufacturing as a whole made rapid progress in Alabama between 1850 and 1860, its total value more than doubling. This is especially significant when the South as a region showed a 7½% decline for the decade.

By 1860 a great variety of products were being made in the state — from ax handles in neighborhood shops to elegant steamboats in the stocks of Meaher's Ship Yard in Mobile. The incomplete manufacturing census of 1860 (several counties failed to report) showed there were 56 different industries in the state and 1,459 manufacturing establishments.[60] The leading counties in the value of manufactured products were Mobile, Madison, Autauga, Baldwin and Tuscaloosa.

The 1860 Census lists Stroup and Alexander as owners and operators of a forge at Tannehill representing a capital investment of $20,000. During the year ending June 1, 1860, census records show 490,000 pounds of iron ore, 20,000 pounds of limestone and 20,000 bushels of coal were consumed producing some 10 tons of iron and 10 tons of castings. The ore cost $245, limestone $10 and coal $900 per ton. The operation employed 40 workers with a monthly payroll of $1,040.[61]

While most historical accounts of ironmaking at Tannehill list charcoal as the fuel source, the census reference to coal leads to speculation that it was being used not only on an experimental basis but, at times, as a mix or substitute. Charcoal, which was locally produced, was not listed as a purchased raw material in the census report. It is also likely that coal was used in reheating iron for castings and in the foundry operation.

The speculation that coal might have been used at Tannehill is also supported by a 1970 analysis done by *Modern Castings Magazine.* "The arsenic and phosphorous contents are typical of irons produced from local ores and the high sulfur content of the cast iron may indicate that the ironmaster may have cheated a little by supplementing his charcoal with a little high sulfur coal from a nearby deposit."[62]

The 1860 Census report may have been filed just as the No. 1 blast furnace at Tannehill was nearing completion. Woodward says the furnace went into blast sometime between 1859 and 1861.

The amount of investment in the operation, $20,000, was five times the amount listed just 10 years earlier in the 1850 Census. That report shows Colonel Tannehill had a capital investment of only $4,000 in the iron operation and employed six workers at a monthly wage outlay of $60.[63]

Although the Tannehill Ironworks is located in Tuscaloosa County near the Jefferson and Bibb County lines, the 1860 Census mistakenly shows it in Bibb.

In 1862 John Alexander sold the ironworks to William L. Sanders (sometimes spelled Saunders) of Marion. Stroup, who remained as superintendent for a few months, moved to Jefferson County and began construction of the Oxmoor Furnace. Oxmoor, the first ironworks to be built in Jefferson County, was almost a copy of Tannehill No. 1. It went into blast in October of 1863.[64]

Meanwhile back at Tannehill, Sanders immediately began to expand the plant to bring its production to 20 tons a day to aid the war effort. On March 23, 1863 he signed a contract with the Nitre and Mining Bureau of the Confederate government to deliver "on the cars of the Alabama and Tennessee River Railroad at Montevallo 4,000 tons of pig iron per annum."[65] From there, the iron would be shipped to the Selma Arsenal. The contract also stipulated that any iron produced in excess of 4,000 tons would also belong to the government.

Apparently Sanders planned for expansion of operations to include hot as well as cold blast. The contract, signed by Lt. Col. I. M. St. John, chief of the Nitre and Mining Bureau, required that "not more than 15% shall be in No. 3 hot or cold blast iron; not more than 35% in No. 2 hot or cold blast iron; and the balance to be in No. 1 hot or cold blast iron."

THE BIG WHEEL AND GEAR WORKS from the steam engine installed by William L. Sanders and Co. using Confederate bonds in 1863 can be seen in this photograph dating to the early 1920s. Parts of the 16-foot wheel are still in existence. (Iron and Steel Musuem of Alabama)

Monthly deliveries were not to fall below 150 tons of iron. For his product, the government contract stipulated the following price schedule:

		Amount Paid
No. 1 Charcoal Cold Blast Pig Iron per ton of 2,240 lbs.	....	$75.00
No. 2 Charcoal Cold Blast Pig Iron per ton of 2,240 lbs.	....	$67.50
No. 3 Charcoal Cold Blast Pig Iron per ton of 2,240 lbs.	....	$62.50
No. 1 Charcoal Hot Blast Pig Iron per ton of 2,240 lbs.	....	$65.00
No. 2 Charcoal Hot Blast Pig Iron per ton of 2,240 lbs.	....	$55.00
No. 3 Charcoal Hot Blast Pig Iron per ton of 2,240 lbs.	....	$50.00

Revealing the effect of inflation and rising prices for provisions and labor, the contract was amended July 1, 1863 stipulating $100 per ton of No. 1 cold blast pig iron, $90 for No. 2 and $75 for No. 3. A similar amendment in 1864 shows the price had risen to $160 per ton for No. 1, $144 for No. 2 and $118 for No. 3.[66]

No mention was made in the amendments of hot blast pig iron indicating perhaps that Sanders was having some trouble making his hot blast stoves operate.

Hot blast equipment on charcoal furnaces was primitive and experimental. It consisted of a blowing engine which forced hot air into the bottom of the furnace. The air was preheated by passing it through a stove consisting of a series of cast iron pipes located at the top of the furnace and heated by the flame coming out the stacks. This method was crude and unsatisfactory since the pipes, subjected to the furnace's flame, lasted but a short time and required frequent replacement.[67]

A Republic Iron and Steel Co. memo dated June 18, 1926 providing an inventory of "all the remaining old parts" of the Tannehill Furnaces lists a great amount of 12-inch pipe, air compressor parts and a furnace stove. Republic later scrapped the relics in its Thomas Furnaces but the inventory confirms hot blast was at least used experimentally at Tannehill.[68]

To help Sanders expand the ironworks, the Nitre and Mining Bureau advanced him $50,000 in Confederate bonds with which he completed Furnaces Nos. 2 and 3 (called the Double Furnaces) and put in a steam engine to replace the old and sometimes unreliable system of water power. The contract made allowances for the difficulties in hauling the iron the 18 miles to the railhead at Montevallo.

"As there is a haul of 18 miles from the works to the point of delivery, and the roads are liable to be so much broken up by bad weather, so that (Sanders) may not be able to deliver the full amount of 1,000 tons per quarter, it is agreed that any excess of iron delivered in any other quarter shall be credited to the quarter in which he may be deficient."[69]

It is doubtful the furnaces at Tannehill, although the only site in Alabama where three of them stood side by side during the Civil War, ever reached its quota.

The trip to Montevallo over the old iron trail was a major undertaking. At least once a day the wagons had to be loaded and the mule or ox

DIORAMA OF THE TANNEHILL IRONWORKS, built for the University of Alabama in 1953 by Thomas H. DeJarnette, Jr., indicates what the furnace operation looked like during the Civil War. Old Tannehill was Alabama's only three-furnace ironmaker. (South Central Bell)

teams harnessed for the trip. To meet his contract of 1,000 tons of pig iron every three months, Sanders would have had to deliver 10 tons of iron a day to Montevallo.[70]

Not only did the war-time ironmakers face labor and production problems, the use of ox carts for transport to railheads severely curtailed their movement over wet roads. Original track for the railroad that now runs near Tannehill, the Alabama Great Southern, was not laid until 1869-1871 by the Alabama & Chattanooga Railroad Company.[71]

In addition to the raw pig iron, which was shipped in ingots, Tannehill produced large quantities of ordnance and other finished products in its own foundry. Armes says the plant operated all during the war "making cannon balls, gun barrels, ordnance, all the munitions of war in addition to pots, pans and skillets for use of the Confederate Army.[72] Some of these relics can be seen today in the Iron and Steel Museum at Tannehill.

While no mention of castings at Tannehill is made in the Confederate contract, their manufacture is clearly in evidence and it is possible they were shipped to other destinations than Selma. What records of shipments Sanders had on file were more than likely destroyed in the Union raid on the furnace site.

Modern Castings reported "numerous direct iron castings produced here from 1855 to 1865" were uncovered in its 1970 study, a process which even bypassed the need for the foundry operation.[73] The University of Alabama archaeological investigation in 1956 also turned up a large collection of castings.

The Confederacy's main interest in Tannehill, however, was in raw pig iron production and as much of it as possible. The contract with Sanders was not set to expire until January 1, 1867 or until the "establishment of peace relations with the United States."

The wording of the contract indicates Sanders had already begun work on Furnaces Nos. 2 and 3 by March of 1863 as the $50,000 in Confederate bonds was for completion of the Double Furnaces.

> "To enable the party of the first part (Sanders) to finish the furnace now under construction, it is agreed that the party of the second part (Confederate government) shall advance to the party of the first part $50,000 in bonds of the Confederate States of America, one-half on the signing and ratification of this contract; one-fourth on the requisition of the party of the first part; and the remaining one-fourth upon a second requisition of the party of the first part . . ."[74]

The Double Furnaces, which in all probability included some hot blast apparatus, were put into blast sometime in 1863. Their hurried war-time construction may have contributed to a crack in the furnace wall some years later. The older Single Furnace showed no similar signs of collapse.

What Union troops found at Tannehill when they arrived on March 31, 1865 was a veritable industrial complex tucked away in the backhills of Roupes Valley.

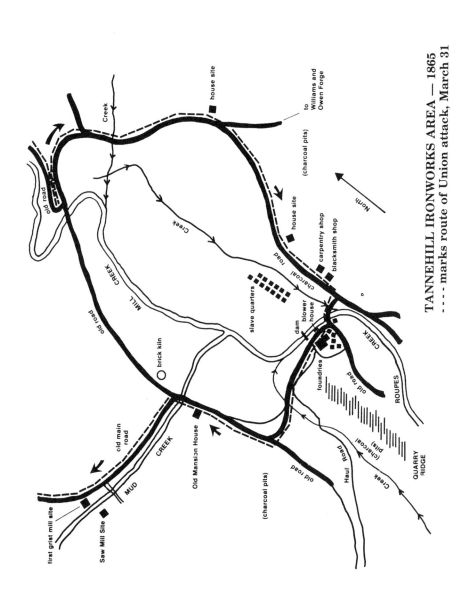

TANNEHILL IRONWORKS AREA — 1865
- - - marks route of Union attack, March 31

Not only did the ironworks keep a number of small blacksmith operations going, probably on both sides of Roupes Creek, the immediate area also supported a gristmill, saw mill and a large tan yard operated by Thomas Lightfoot Williams which made saddles and harness for the Confederacy.

Williams and Thomas Hennington Owen also operated a forge one mile south of the Tannehill Furnaces on Roupes Creek, the product of which, like Tannehill's, went to the Confederate government by way of rail out of Montevallo. It is likely some of the "finished products" produced of Tannehill pig iron were made at the Williams and Owen Forge just over the line in Bibb County.

Hidden even deeper in the back country, the forge escaped the federal attack but was washed away by a flood in 1866. Not being ironmakers themselves, Owen and Williams hired an expert iron worker from Tennessee, Thomas C. Bratton, to build and operate the forge.

Owen was best known as a planter and merchant in Jefferson County where he served as county commissioner in the late 1870s.

Located just below a wide shoals in Roupes Creek, the old forge was noted for turning out pieces of hardware including nails, horseshoes and harness gear. Little remains of the site today except for scattered stones on the south side of the creek where the forge and another tannery were located. Remnants of heavy stonework which supported a roadway on the north side from which ran a supply road from the Tannehill Furnaces are also clearly evident.

Iron pins can still be found in the roadway support where rock is stacked in places eight and 10 feet high. An excavation by the Iron and Steel Museum late in 1985 uncovered a number of artifacts.

"They didn't do all this work just for a road," says Clarence Sellers, Scout Master of Hueytown Boy Scout Troop 207, who found the forge site in 1975. "This was a well planned operation."[75]

Overshadowed by the much larger ironworks at Tannehill, little mention of the Williams and Owen Forge has been included in the written history of the state.

The big group of furnaces at Tannehill was supplied with skilled labor from the Army, a practice no doubt aimed at insuring the Confederacy's investment as well as to keep check on production. Others who worked in iron mills, foundries and factories in the state considered critical to the Confederate cause were exempt from military duty. There is no doubt, however, that in sites like Tannehill slaves made up the larger part of the work force.

Army conscripts deserted just as they did from regular ranks. On June 14, 1864 Sanders wrote his counterpart at the Shelby Ironworks located some 17 miles east of Montevallo, the following:

"Gleason, an Irishman by birth, by trade a blacksmith, age about 40 years and being attached to me, has deserted. If he should apply at your works for employment, please refuse him and inform me."[76]

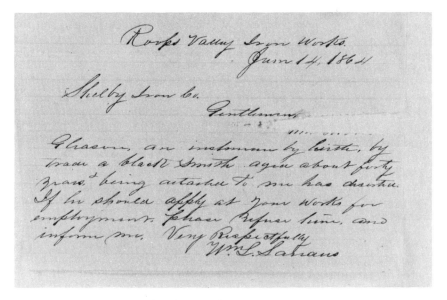

LETTER by William L. Sanders written from Tannehill June 14, 1864 to Shelby Iron Company. The original is a part of the W. L. Chew Papers at the Samford University Library.

PART OF ROCK RETAINING WALL, last remnant of Williams and Owen Forge near Tannehill. (Ed Nelson)

Under Confederate law it would have been unlawful for Shelby to hire Gleason once the superintendent knew he was assigned to Sanders at Tannehill.

To discourage one ironworks from hiring workers of another, which with a shortage of skilled labor was a temptation, the Selma office of the Nitre and Mining Bureau issued the following bulletin during the latter part of June, 1863:

"In accordance with General Orders, No. 30 and 32, A. & I. Office, the following regulations will be observed by contractors with this bureau.

1. All detailed men and conscripts leaving their work or refusing to work, will at once be turned over to the nearest Enrolling Officer to be tried and punished as deserters.

2. Any contractor hiring the operatives of another contractor, without his written consent, will be immediately reported to this office; and if the operative so employed is not at once discharged or returned to his employer, all detailed men and conscripts will be at once removed from the works of the offending party, and such other action taken as will effectually prevent a practice so destructive to the interest of all.

3. No subsequent employment of the operative, so discharged, will be permitted without the consent of the original employer be first obtained.

4. No transfer of detailed men or conscripts from one contractor to another will be permitted, even with the consent of all parties until such transfer is first approved by the Officer in charge. The Major in command will use all the power with which he is clothed to prevent interference with the employees of one contractor by another, either by the offer of higher wages or otherwise. It is a practice eminently calculated to destroy the whole iron interest, and it is hoped iron masters will not resort to such devices."[77]

WM. RICHARDSON HUNT
Major &c on Ord. Duty, in charge of Iron
and Mining of Ala., Ga., & Tenn.

Iron companies under contract to the Confederacy were almost like military outposts. In many cases the heads of the companies were given military commissions as officers and the skilled men as non-commissioned officers.

While slave labor provided the bulk of the work force (a Confederate report for 1864 showed the cost of "Negro hire" at $300 per year),[78] skilled white supervisors in a typical plant would include the superintendent, the moulders and the men in charge of mining and charcoal operations.

Also each plant had agents who devoted full time to foraging for supplies including food such as meat and corn, and hay for horses, mules and oxen. Lack of labor and supplies shut down furnaces for weeks at a time.

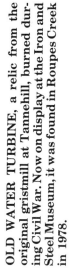

OLD WATER TURBINE, a relic from the original gristmill at Tannehill, burned during Civil War. Now on display at the Iron and Steel Museum, it was found in Roupes Creek in 1978.

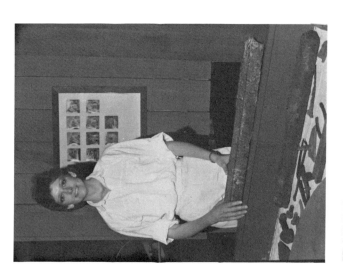

IRON INGOTS made at Tannehill were stamped "Roupes Valley Ironworks" and shipped to Selma during the war period. A number are on display at the Iron and Steel Museum at Tannehill. Pictured is Vicki Gentry, museum curator. (Joe Aloia)

Labor and foodstuffs were not the only problems furnace operators faced. Inflation also drove the prices up and the price of iron rose accordingly.

Prior to the war in 1860, Tannehill pig iron sold for $17.40 a ton. A price schedule for 1864, however, showed Tannehill No. 1 cold blast pig iron had risen to $160 a ton, more than double the rate for the previous year.[79] As the war progressed and the credit of the Confederacy weakened, the price of iron per ton in Alabama rose to $500. In contrast, pig iron in the North during the same period was selling for $73.50 a ton. That the war had a stimulating effect on the iron industry in Alabama, despite the high inflation rate, is undeniable.

Gov. A. B. Moore, in his message to the Legislature on October 28, 1861, said:

> "Mechanical arts and industrial pursuits, hitherto practically unknown to our people, are already in operation. The clink of the hammer and the busy hum of the workshop are beginning to be heard throughout the land. Our manufactories are rapidly increasing and the inconvenience which would result from the continuances of the war and the closing of our ports for years would be more than compensated by forcing us to the development of our abundant resources, and the tone and the temper it would give to our national character. Under such circumstances the return of peace would find us a self-reliant and truly independent people."[80]

Moore's prophecy might have been true enough had the war ended in 1864 without the destruction that was to follow. By late 1864 and 1865 most of Alabama's industries lay in shambles.

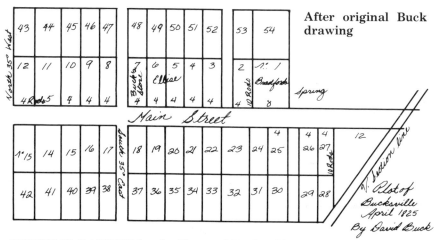

ORIGINAL LAYOUT for the Town of Bucksville, drawn 1825 by David Buck. Main Street was also the Old Huntsville Road. (From private papers of Delores Smith, Bucksville)

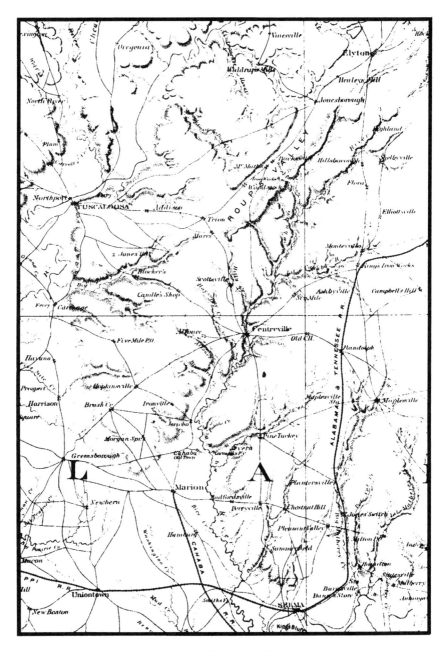

WEST CENTRAL ALABAMA IN 1865. Note the prominence given Roupes Valley, the Tannehill Ironworks near Bucksville and routes to Tuscaloosa and Selma. (From Atlas, War of the Rebellion, U.S. War Department)

CHAPTER IV

WAR BRINGS A TERRIBLE TOLL

*". . . the South for a whole generation had been making a valiant attempt
to reject the industrial revolution, and this attempt had involved it at last
in a war in which the industrial revolution would be the decisive factor."*

> — Bruce Catton
> (The American Heritage History of the
> Civil War, 1960)

As storm clouds gathered over the South in the closing months of the
Civil War, Tannehill braced itself for what would be almost certain
destruction.

Already two Union raids had been made into Alabama. The first,
commanded by Col. A. D. Streight, began April 19, 1863 and took 2,000
picked troops through the mountain region of North Alabama from
Colbert County toward Rome, Georgia, site of the Noble Brothers
Foundry. Streight surrendered to Nathan Bedford Forrest's Confederates before he reached the Georgia border.

Gen. Lovell H. Rousseau led 2,300 men on a second raid through
Alabama from Decatur southeast through Calhoun County and Talladega and on to Lee County beginning July 10, 1864. This operation
would have more serious consequences. Cane Creek Furnace and the
unfinished Janney Furnace, both near Anniston, were destroyed during
Rousseau's attack.

Neither foray, however, would come close to the devastation caused by
the third. Maj. Gen. James H. Wilson, with 14,000 seasoned troops
rested over the winter, decamped from near Gravelly Springs in
Lauderdale County March 20-22, 1865 and headed south.

Some 12,000 of his troops were armed with new seven-shot Spencer
repeating carbines and 120 rounds of ammunition. The invading force,
12,500 cavalry and 1,500 dismounted men, included 36 batteries of
12-pounder cannon, 58 pontoons and 60 supply wagons divided into
three divisions commanded by Brig. Gens. Edward M. McCook, Eli Long
and Emory Upton.[81]

While his movement was designed in part to divert Confederate
attention from Union plans to attack Mobile, Wilson's main objective
was to destroy Alabama's ironworks, factories and mines and to wreck
the huge Selma Arsenal.

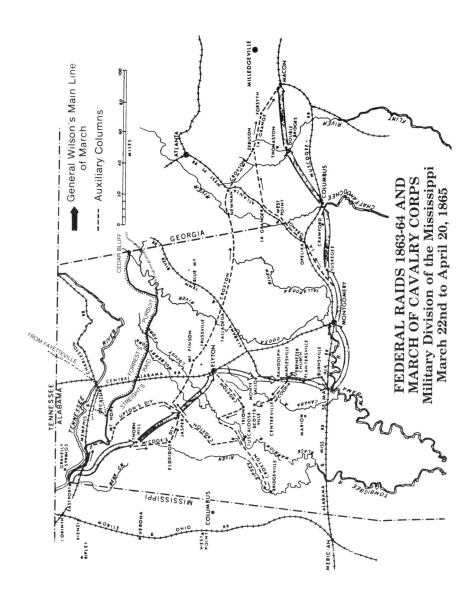

FEDERAL RAIDS 1863-64 AND
MARCH OF CAVALRY CORPS
Military Division of the Mississippi
March 22nd to April 20, 1865

Union strategists hoped the massive raid into central Alabama would topple the staggering Confederate government by taking away its manufacturing base and source of war materials.

Wilson, who had recently distinguished himself as the reorganizer of the U.S. Cavalry, ordered his troops to re-unite at Elyton in Jefferson County where he made his headquarters at Arlington Mansion on March 29.

Brig. Gen. John T. Croxton, Commander of the First Brigade, was detached from McCook's Division and with 1,500 men sent to attack Tuscaloosa, site of the University of Alabama. Wilson, himself, led the main federal force toward Selma by way of Montevallo. Hopefully, the two columns would meet again in the vicinity of Centreville.

In actuality there was little resistance to Wilson's Raid through Alabama. Old men and boys were no match for his well-equipped army while most of Alabama's fighting men had been involved in engagements in other states, mainly Virginia and Tennessee.

While Cane Creek and Janney Furnaces had become the first Alabama ironworks to fall before the Union advance in 1864, Maj. Gen. Francis B. Blair Jr., moving his 17th Corps from the west to reinforce Sherman in Atlanta, came across the Round Mountain and Cornwall Furnaces in Cherokee County in the summer of the same year and laid them in ruin.

Wilson, however, would put five furnaces out of commission, laying in waste Little Cahaba and Brierfield — along with its rolling mill — in Bibb County, the Shelby Furnaces in Shelby County and Oxmoor and Irondale in Jefferson County during March and April, 1865.

Croxton's forces, which had split from Wilson's at Elyton, attacked the Tannehill Ironworks, also known as Sanders or Saunders Ironworks, on their way to Tuscaloosa March 31. Marching to rejoin Wilson in Georgia in April (the link-up with Wilson at Centreville never took place), Croxton's men also put the torch to Oxford, Jenifer and Knight Furnaces. Only the furnace of Hale and Murdock in Lamar County escaped Union detection along with some small forges.

Alabama was a logical target. Its 15 producing ironworks gave it special prominence, even more so in the later years of the war. Although the exact tonnage is not known, Alabama furnaces produced more iron for the Confederacy than all other Southern states combined.[82]

That the iron industry in Alabama had been given a boost by the war effort was evidenced by the fact that in 1860, the year before the outbreak of hostilities, the state had only six iron furnaces in operation representing a total capital investment of $225,000. That represented only 12 per cent of the total for the South and less than one per cent of the total for the nation. Alabama iron production in 1860 amounted to 1,742 tons, five per cent of the South's total output and .1 per cent of the nation's.[83]

At the war's end in 1865, however, Alabama could boast of 43 iron manufactories including 20 high furnaces at 16 plants, 17 forges and six rolling mills.

Maj. Gen. James H. Wilson, USA
(Library of Congress)

Brig. Gen. John T. Croxton, USA
(Library of Congress)

Lt. Gen. Nathan Bedford
Forrest, CSA
(Alabama Dept. of Archives
and History)

Brig. Gen. Josiah Gorgas, CSA

(University of Alabama)

Late in 1864, due to reversals on the battlefield and lost territory elsewhere in the Confederacy, Alabama was producing 70% of the South's iron supply.[84]

Only four years before, Tennessee had been the leading Southern iron producer with 17 furnaces that smelted 22,302 tons annually, and Virginia led in the manufacture of bar iron, sheet metal and railroad iron.[85]

As the war spread, the Confederacy began to depend more heavily on the lower South, particularly Alabama. Locations of various new ironworks in Alabama had closely followed Tuomey's published records of where ore deposits could be found. Using such information, Gen. Josiah Gorgas, Confederate chief in ordnance, was able to help plot Alabama's partial change-over from a cotton to an industrial war economy which made the state "the Arsenal of the Confederacy."

Between 1861 and 1865 the South mined more than 150,000 tons of iron ore of which there is official record. Alabama's furnaces are credited with producing 30,000 tons of pig iron annually and 10,000 tons of bars.[86]

During the first year of the war in 1861, the South had depended heavily on munitions shipped from Europe and South America, but beginning in 1862 it realized, as Union blockades became more effective, military needs would have to rely more on home production.

With the decision to bolster its own manufacturing, the Confederacy on April 11, 1862 established the Nitre and Mining Bureau to encourage local production of war materials and other necessities for its various arsenals.

At the start of hostilities Alabama's six existing furnaces probably were producing less than 40 tons daily, a large part of that coming from Little Cahaba No. 1, Shelby No. 1 and Tannehill No. 1.

The iron shortage became so severe that the Confederate Congress on June 16, 1863 passed an act empowering the Nitre and Mining Bureau to impress all private manufacturing. Plants that refused "forced sale" of their products to the government ran the very real risk of being confiscated. In return, plant managers were given funding to expand their operations, in many cases up to 50% of the capital needs outlay.

While it is safe to assume many of its advances were never repaid, the Confederate Congress, in passing the assistance act April 19, 1862, set up a liberal repayment plan where interest free loans could be paid back in products received. In addition, contracts for iron and coal could run as long as six years.[87]

Between 1862 and 1865 thirteen new blast furnaces were built in Alabama with the government advancing either all or part of the funds for these operations.

The Bureau had originally been created to insure adequate supplies of saltpeter for making gunpowder. Its powers, however, were extended a year later to cover iron, coal, lead, copper and zinc.

REPORT OF CHIEF OF NITRE AND MINING BUREAU.

CONFEDERATE STATES OF AMERICA,
WAR DEPARTMENT,
NITRE AND MINING BUREAU,
Richmond, Va., Jan. 31, 1865.

HON. JAMES A. SEDDON, *Secretary of War:*

SIR:

In reply to the enclosed resolution of enquiry, I have the honor to state—

1st. Seven (7) iron furnaces and one (1) forge were worked, in the year 1864, by officers and agents of the government and on government account, under the direction of this Bureau, viz: three (3) furnaces in Virginia, two (2) furnaces in Alabama, with one rolling mill, and the usual complement of puddling and heating fires: and in the Trans-Mississippi, two (2) furnaces and two (2) forges.

2d. The "cost per ton of pig, bloom and bar iron, respectively, at such furnaces and forges," is given, as closely as can now be ascertained. in the enclosed tabulated statement A, in Virginia, with precision; from Alabama, by telegraph, and probably approximately; from the Trans-Mississippi, accounts have not yet been received.

It will be noted that the Virginia furnaces have been worked with all the interruptions of war—from the actual presence of the enemy to the impressment of supplies by our own forces. In Alabama the government furnaces have been worked in an abundant country, and almost with peace regularity.

3d. The number of iron furnaces and forges worked in the same time by the proprietors, under contract, are given in statement B. The different forms of contract so made are indicated by the general forms C and D, used by the Bureau: the first, where advances of government funds have been made to contractors, and the last, where not. More precise information can only be given, by submitting the contracts in bulk.

It is proper here to state, that to stimulate production by private interest, and to throw upon the market an additional quantity of iron for agriculture and the rail roads, the Bureau policy has been to require from each furnace only so much iron as the military requisitions exact—ranging from fifty (50) per cent. where no government advance has been made, to ~~~~ per cent. where advances have been made, v ~~~~ al

PAGE FROM CSA IMPRINT, survey of Southern iron supply, issued at request of Confederate House of Representatives.

Several improvements were added during the war years to increase iron production including replacement of water-powered blowers with steam engines as was the case at Tannehill; raw bituminous coal was substituted for charcoal at Shelby; and coke was substituted for charcoal at Irondale. A manually operated bell and hopper was installed on top of Shelby No. 1 in 1863 marking its first use on an Alabama furnace, and hot blast stoves were also first installed here.

That the South was slow to change to more modern technology in iron production is well documented. Alabama furnaces were still using charcoal as the heating source while northern ironworks were being converted to coal. English ironmakers had abandoned the process decades earlier.

A letter written from the Shelby Iron Company to Confederate Sen. Charles B. Mitchell April 26, 1864 as to Alabama iron production said experiments with coal at the Shelby plant proved iron of superior quality could be made using raw coal as fuel.

"The result of this experiment was every way satisfactory," wrote Shelby's president, A. T. Jones.[88]

Warning that the South was pursuing a "wrong policy" as to charcoal use, he said the small iron production derived from it hardly justified the destruction of Alabama forests "especially with such great reserves of coal in the area."

Jones said original plans were to expand the Shelby works to as many as five blast furnaces using charcoal, but so much time was required to operate the one built in 1863 (Shelby No. 2) the idea was dropped. From March, 1863 to March, 1864 the Shelby works produced about 3,500 tons. Although the amount appeared small, he added, it "exceeds what any other company in this state made within the same period."

While Jones said Shelby had planned to shift completely to coal, a plan he predicted would increase production 100 per cent, and with less labor, the war shut down the plant before the change-over could be made.

The Jones report said Alabama iron production for the 12 months from March 1863 to March 1864 was "probably less than 10 tons." If five of them were converted to coal, he predicted, production would double.[89]

Although coke had been used in English furnaces for over a hundred years, as early as 1856 21 blast furnaces in Pennsylvania and three in Maryland had already made the change. Interestingly enough coal had been mined in Alabama for over 40 years at this time and coke had been made for foundry use in Tuscaloosa in 1854.[90]

The raw material support the various ironworks provided the Selma Arsenal is well documented. Iron from the interior went into naval plate, field cannon and shells and all the munitions of war.

"Indeed the story of the Tredegar Ironworks in Richmond and the arsenal and foundry at Selma are well known as the backbone of the

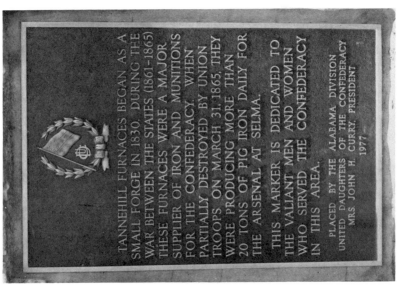

TANNEHILL FURNACES BEGAN AS A
SMALL FORGE IN 1830. DURING THE
WAR BETWEEN THE STATES (1861–1865)
THESE FURNACES WERE A MAJOR
SUPPLIER OF IRON AND MUNITIONS
FOR THE CONFEDERACY. WHEN
PARTIALLY DESTROYED BY UNION
TROOPS ON MARCH 31, 1865, THEY
WERE PRODUCING MORE THAN
20 TONS OF PIG IRON DAILY FOR
THE ARSENAL AT SELMA.

THIS MARKER IS DEDICATED TO
THE VALIANT MEN AND WOMEN
WHO SERVED THE CONFEDERACY
IN THIS AREA.

PLACED BY THE ALABAMA DIVISION
UNITED DAUGHTERS OF THE CONFEDERACY
MRS JOHN H. CURRY, PRESIDENT
1977

Confederate Memorial at Tannehill dedicated 1977

Confederate ordnance department," said the late Milo B. Howard, Jr., director of the Alabama Department of Archives and History from 1967 to 1981. "But backing up these sprawling operations were the suppliers of iron and supplementing them were small furnaces and forges in mineral regions of the interior of the Confederacy.

"Tannehill Furnace exemplified the nascent iron industry in the South which helped to provide iron and ordnance which made the long continuation of the war possible."[91]

Howard, who died in 1981, said in dedication ceremonies for the Daughters of the Confederacy Marker at Tannehill October 26, 1977, that Roupes Valley had been a "beehive" of military activity and represented "an important segment in the growing self-sufficiency of the Confederate government."

The following Alabama furnaces supplied pig iron to the Confederacy during the five-year course of the war:

	Furnaces	Blown In	Daily Capacity/ Tons
1. Cane Creek (Calhoun County)	1	1840	8
2. Little Cahaba (Bibb County)	2	1848/1863	12
3. Shelby (Shelby County)	2	1849/1863	15
4. Round Mountain (Cherokee County)	1	1852	12
5. Hale and Murdock (Lamar County)	1	1859	11
6. Tannehill (Tuscaloosa County)	3	1859/1863	20
7. Brierfield (Bibb County)	2	1861/1863	25
8. Jackson (Jackson County)	1	1861	8
9. Rock Run (Cherokee County)	1	(unknown)	14
10. Cornwall (Cherokee County)	1	1862	6
11. Oxford (Calhoun County)	1	1863	15
12. Oxmoor (Jefferson County)	1	1863	20
13. Jenifer (Talladega County)	1	1863	10
14. Knight (Talladega County)	1	1863	8
15. Irondale (Jefferson County)	1	1863	20

Janney in Calhoun County was hit while under construction in 1864. It had one furnace with a daily capacity of 15 tons.

This list, a compilation from records of both Armes and Woodward, does not include numerous foundries, bloomeries and blacksmith operations frequently called "ironworks."

Armes also lists six rolling mills as being in operation in Alabama during the war years, Shelby, Brierfield, Saunders and the Alabama Rolling Mill, each with a 10 ton daily capacity, Helena with 15 and Selma with 30.

In the category of "other" types of iron businesses fell the Williams and Owen Forge near Tannehill, which escaped Union detection, and the Mt. Pinson Ironworks on the banks of Turkey Creek in Jefferson County. A Tennessean named McGee, together with slaves trained as blacksmiths, erected a small forge and foundry at this site in 1863. Although McGee had more ambitious plans, the operation became little more than a blacksmith shop overrun by demands for horseshoes by Confederates on the move.[92]

OXMOOR FURNACES after being rebuilt in 1873. Note iron furnace tops on stone base at left center of this early woodcut. (Woodward, Alabama Blast Furnaces)

IRONDALE FURNACE as it appeared in 1873. In this rare photo, note the long wooden trestle over Shades Creek in foreground. (George Gordon Crawford Papers, Samford University Library)

Reports from the Nitre and Mining Bureau indicated the capacity of Alabama furnaces was seldom reached and that the average per furnace was closer to four tons a day. It is a matter of record that from January 1, 1863 to September 30, 1864, Alabama furnaces sent to the Confederacy only 12,354 gross tons and from January 1, 1864 to September 30, 1864, a somewhat disappointing 5,913 tons.[93]

"In one case, the government furnace in Bibb County, Alabama, averaged through the month 13 tons of iron per day, and at another furnace an average of 10 tons per day was obtained for one month. From many disturbing causes incident to the war much time has been lost at the Alabama furnaces and the daily average would scarcely exceed, if equal, four tons per day."[94]

As the war progressed the number of Alabama furnaces decreased as they fell victim to Union attack. A report from Secretary of War John C. Breckinridge to President Jefferson Davis on February 17, 1865 lists only nine Alabama iron furnaces as being under contract with the Confederacy:

Contractor	Name of Works	County
J. B. Knight & Company	Chockolocco Furnace (Knight)	Talladega
Oxford Iron Company	Oxford Iron Works	Calhoun
Shelby Iron Company	Shelby Iron Works	Shelby
W. L. Ward & Company	Little Cahaba	Bibb
W. L. Sanders	Roopes Valley Iron Works (Tannehill)	Jefferson
W. S. McElwain	Cahawba Iron Works (Irondale)	Jefferson
S. Clabaugh & Company	Salt Creek Iron Works (Jenifer)	Talladega
Daughdrill & Creigher	Round Mountain Iron Works	Cherokee
Red Mountain Iron & Coal Company	Red Mountain Iron Works (Oxmoor)	Jefferson[95]

Interestingly enough, in this report, Tannehill (also referred to as Roopes (sic) Valley Iron Works) is listed as being in Jefferson County when it actually is located in Tuscaloosa County near the Jefferson and Bibb County lines.

A tenth Alabama iron producer is also mentioned in the Breckinridge report, the Bibb Furnaces (also known as the Brierfield of Bibb Naval Furnaces) in a listing of iron plants worked by the government. As mentioned earlier in this volume, Brierfield had been confiscated by the Confederate government in 1863 — along with its rolling mill — from private interests unwilling to sign a government contract. Brierfield was the only Alabama furnace listed as government operated.

While many of the Alabama furnaces had small foundries attached to them, most of the iron they produced went to Confederate arsenals at either Selma, Alabama or Rome, Georgia.

By 1864 Selma had not only become Alabama's leading industrial city, it could boast of the largest ordnance depot in the Confederate

CONFEDERATE NAVAL FOUNDRY MONUMENT in Selma marks the location of the old Navy Yard and ordnance works, once the largest in the South. (Jackie Barker)

states. One-half of the cannon and two-thirds of the fixed ammunition used by the South during the last two years of the war were made here.[96]

Next to the Tredegar Ironworks of Richmond, Virginia, the greatest iron manufacturing center in the Confederacy was at Selma. Colin McRae had erected a foundry here under contract with the Confederacy to cast cannon in 1861. When he sold it to the government two years later, the Confederacy developed it into a huge ordnance center including an arsenal, powder works and naval foundry including more than 100 buildings. At peak production, the government operations and private factories at Selma covered 50 acres and employed 6,000 men. It was the only site in the South that could cast heavy artillery of the Brooke Cannon class (15 inches).[97]

The huge complex, which Union troops would compare to northern installations at St. Louis and Philadelphia, underwent a major expansion in 1862 when Gen. Gorgas moved the arsenal at Mt. Vernon, Alabama to Selma for better protection.[98]

Everything was manufactured here "for the soldiers in the field from a horseshoe nail to a cannon carriage."[99] So were the large battleships, the Tennessee, Gaines and Morgan.

To provide some insight into the enormity of the operations at Selma by 1865, the following was included in a report from Brig. Gen. Edward F. Winslow to whom the assignment was given by the federals after the attack on Selma to destroy "everything which could be of benefit to the enemy."

1. Selma Arsenal — Consisting of 24 buildings, containing an immense amount of war material and machinery for manufacturing the same. Very little of the machinery had been removed, although much of it was packed and ready for shipment to Macon and Columbus, Georgia. Among other articles here destroyed were 15 siege guns and 10 heavy carriages, 10 field pieces with 60 field carriages, 10 caissons, 63,000 rounds of artillery ammunition, one million rounds of small arms ammunition, three million feet of lumber, 10,000 bushels of coal, 300 barrels resin and three large engines and boilers.
2. Government Naval Foundry — Consisting of five large buildings, containing three fire engines, 13 boilers, 29 siege guns, unfinished, and all the machinery necessary to manufacture on a large scale naval and siege guns.
3. Selma Iron Works — Consisting of five buildings, with five large engines and furnaces, and complete machinery.
4. Pierce's Foundry, Nos. 1 and 2 — Each of these contained an engine, extensive machinery, and a large lot of tools.
5. Nitre Works — These works consist of 18 buildings, five furnaces, 16 leaches and 90 banks.
6. Powder Mills and Magazine — Consisting of seven buildings, 6,000 rounds of artillery ammunition and 70,000 rounds small arms ammunition, together with 14,000 pounds powder.

"REBEL LOVE," a full-length motion picture shot at Tannehill in 1983, used the park's historic setting in scenes depicting Braxton Bragg's Perryville Campaign. (Raven Cliff Productions)

7. Washington Works — Small iron works, with one engine.
8. Tennessee Iron Works — Containing two engines.
9. Phelan and McBride's Machine Shop, with two engines.
10. Horse Shoe Manufactory — Containing one engine; about 8,000 pounds of horse shoes from this establishment were used by our army.
11. Selma Shovel Factory — This factory contained one steam engine, eight forges and complete machinery for manufacturing shovels, railroad spikes and iron axle-trees for army wagons.
12. On the Alabama and Mississippi Railroad — One roundhouse, one stationary engine and much standing machinery, together with 20 box and two passenger cars.
13. On the Tennessee Railroad — One roundhouse with machinery, five locomotives, one machine, 19 box and 50 platform cars.
14. In the fortifications — one thirty-pound, four ten-pound guns, 11 field pieces, 10 caissons, two forges, and 500 rounds of fixed ammunition . . .[100]

Wilson's attack was as complete as it was swift. In its wake smoldered the remains of a ruined industrial economy on which the state had pegged its hopes for the future.

Says Armes: "The burning went on and on — and beyond that burning city (Selma) smoked the ruins of Oxmoor, Irondale, Tannehill, Brighthope (Little Cahaba), Brierfield, Shelby and all the rest — the coal and iron business of Alabama, quieted now, it seemed forever."[101]

Tannehill's destruction on March 31, 1865 was typical of the quick federal action which left the Alabama iron trade in shambles.

With the federals well-equipped at Elyton and ready to move, Wilson sent Croxton with 1,500 men toward Tuscaloosa while he accompanied his main force toward Selma.

Croxton's command consisted of the Eighth Iowa, Second Michigan, Sixth Kentucky and the Fourth Kentucky mounted infantry.

After leaving Elyton March 30 Croxton marched eight miles before making camp along Eastern Valley Road which he described as being almost impassable. Early the next morning Croxton sent three companies of the Eighth Iowa under Capt. William A. Sutherland to the left to attack the Tannehill Ironworks and Williams Tannery. Another detachment was sent to destroy the stores in Jonesboro.

Croxton's official military report of the attack on Tannehill was simple and to the point:

"Moved at daylight (March 31), sending a detachment to the right through Jonesborough to destroy the stores there, and three companies of the Eighth Iowa, in charge of Capt. Sutherland, my assistant adjutant-general, to the left six miles to destroy Saunders Iron-Works, which they accomplished, rejoining the column five miles south of Bucksville and 10 (miles) from Trion."[102]

HOGAN HOUSE (1834), pioneer home of Archibald and Jane Caffee Hogan, re-located from near Bibbville, Bibb County, at Tannehill Historical State Park in 1972, on site of the old "Mansion House." Note the original rock wall and steps from the "Mansion House" days.

When Sutherland arrived at Tannehill he found Furnaces Nos. 2 and 3 still filled with their molten charge. Before the day was done, his men had put all three furnaces out of commission, blown up the overhead charging bridges, torn up the tramway to the Goethite Mines and set fire to the foundry and cast houses. Passing to the settlement beyond, they razed it including a big tannery that made saddles and harness for the Confederate Army.

Very little escaped the torch, two notable exceptions being the old Tannehill House between the ironworks and Bucksville and the so-called "Mansion House" where Mr. Sanders and his wife, Ann, might have lived. After the war, Giles Edwards lived here. Going up in smoke were numerous industrial buildings, the grist mill, saw mill, even the slave quarters. (On the site of the old "Mansion House," the state relocated the Hogan House (1834) as part of the preservation work at Tannehill Historical State Park in 1972.) An original rock wall, three to four feet high and over 150 feet in length, can still be seen in front of the Mansion House site.

If there was any resistance at Tannehill, Sutherland made no mention of it. Plant workers apparently had been notified of the approach of Union troops and had made for the surrounding countryside and its thick forest cover.

Despite the impending attack, Sanders apparently was planning to get one last run out before the Union raiders arrived. Legend has it that Mary Gordon Duffee, who is quoted earlier in this reference, was hiding in the attic of Arlington Plantation near Elyton where she overheard Wilson order the destruction of the works at Tannehill. The story says she rode horseback and even walked a part of the way, a distance of 25 miles, to warn that the federals were coming. Whether there is any truth to the story, there is no doubt Miss Duffee was well acquainted with the ironworks in Roupes Valley.

As a child in the decade before the Civil War, she traveled through Bucksville in the immediate vicinity of Tannehill on numerous occasions. After the war, she would recount her trips in a series of 59 separate articles from 1885 to 1887 published in the *Birmingham Weekly Iron Age*. The articles would provide a rare insight into pre-war Alabama including glimpses of Tannehill's beginnings and ultimate demise at the hands of Wilson's Raiders.

The fact that Sanders knew the Yankee cavalry was on its way is fairly certain.

George Monlux, an Iowa trooper in Company I, Eighth Iowa Cavalry, said when they arrived at Tannehill no workers were in sight, they apparently having taken the horses and mules into the woods.

Although other official reports indicate Sutherland took three companies of Iowa Cavalry to attack Tannehill, Monlux said only two were detached, Company I under Capt. Elliott Shurtz and Company D under Capt. Lovene Hopkins. The third company may have been used to reconnoiter the area.

GEORGE MONLUX
. .. in later life

HISTORICAL MARKER —
Tannehill

TANNEHILL NOS. 2 and 3 — In this early photo, probably taken around 1900, note wooden ladder which may have been left by persons scavaging bricks from the draft stacks. (Iron and Steel Museum)

Monlux's eyewitness account of the raid on Tannehill is as follows:
"During the day Company I and Company D were ordered off to the left of the line to burn a large iron works and smelter. I was on the advance of this party and as we rode up to the works there was a large collection of colored ladies in front of a building, and one of them addressed me saying, 'What are you all guine to do?' I told her we were going to burn the iron works. She replied, 'I am powerful glad of that for it uses up any amount of niggers every year.'

"Not one white man or a negro was in sight, for they had heard of our coming and the negro men and horses and mules had been run off.

"These works were of great size and must have covered more than an acre of ground, and near the buildings were tens of thousands of bushels of charcoal.

"The boys started fires in several places in the building and as it was built of pitch pine the flames spread so rapidly that some of the boys came near being burned before they could get out. We watched the building and these large piles of charcoal until they were well on the way to destruction when we started on to intercept the column . . ."[103]

It is apparent from Monlux's account, the Iowa soldiers approached the ironworks from the Farley Field area off Eastern Valley Road and left down the old road paralleling but across the creek from the present day main entrance road into Tannehill Historical State Park.

After watching the fires at Tannehill burn out of control, they left the area and "bearing to the right" hit the main road (the Old Huntsville Road) near Bucksville. Arriving ahead of the main column, they came upon a house, corn crib and smoke house and proceeded to appropriate the supplies.

Monlux said after waiting a time for Croxton's main body of troops to arrive, the Iowans were almost mistaken for Confederates before the two forces rejoined.

Sutherland had ordered "a file of men" to go back on the main road to see what was delaying the column.

"A few rods back on the road was a rise of ground, and as the sergeant came up on one side of this raise, the advance guard of the column came up on the other side, and as the advance knew nothing of us being out there in the advance they fired a volley at the sergeant, and the balls came singing over us. Our horses were bridled and eating corn, but when the boys started for their horses the captain (Sutherland) ordered, 'steady there boys, let your horses go and deploy about these buildings. It is probably our advance, but if it is rebels we will stand them off from these buildings.' "

Monlux said it was soon discovered to be Croxton's column "which proceeded on and we waited for our regiment to come along and took our position in the ranks."

Later in the afternoon enroute to Tuscaloosa, Croxton's column, with the Fourth Kentucky in advance, did encounter Roddy's Confederates near Trion (Vance).

Another Iowa soldier who took part in the Tannehill raid was A. S. Ruby of Company D. While Ruby's letters to Alabama historian James A. Anderson in 1934 did not mention the furnace action, he did write of dining with a Methodist preacher during the attack on Tuscaloosa four days later.

"I furnished him one or two *Northwestern Christian Advocates* I had with me that were published in Chicago. He seemed very glad to get them, but rebuked me for coming down there to kill them. I defended myself as best I could, telling him we were just down there to help sustain the federal government."[104]

Ruby, who was 25 at the time, contended most of Croxton's brigade were "westerners," not Yankees, and were not as intent on punishing the South as might have been eastern troops. (Croxton's force was made up mostly of soldiers from Iowa, Michigan and Kentucky).

Although Monlux and Ruby were in separate companies, the two men apparently knew each other. When the brigade crossed the Warrior River, Monlux said they found it difficult to cross.

"Rubee (sic) of Company D was a large heavy man and his brother was much smaller and more active and when he came to this ford the large Rubee gave the lead strap of his horse to his brother and dismounting took his horse by the tail and waded across the river."[105]

Although Croxton, who was only 28, found no opposition of strength along his march from Elyton to Jonesboro and on to Bucksville, he did encounter a sizeable Confederate force near Vance, some 10 miles from the Tannehill Ironworks.

Traveling down the old Huntsville Road, Croxton came across Gen. William H. (Red) Jackson's division which had split away from Forrest's main force to block the federal advance toward Selma.

Forrest, himself, raced on toward Centreville and Selma to defend the huge Confederate Arsenal from Wilson's larger army.

Croxton mistook Jackson's force of about 3,500 men for Forrest's main column of over 10,000 and decided to withdraw to the north to take another route to Tuscaloosa.

Jackson, moving toward Centreville to rejoin Forrest, attacked Croxton's rear guard on April 1, commencing the little battle of Trion. The old Trion community is now known as Vance.

In all some 45 to 50 men were killed or wounded on both sides amounting to more of a skirmish than a full-fledged battle. Nonetheless it was listed in N. A. Strait's *Battles of the War of the Rebellion* published in 1882.

With Croxton in retreat 10 miles back in the direction of Woodstock and Bucksville, Jackson reported he had hopefully scattered the Union force in the woods and saved Tuscaloosa. Jackson then moved toward Centreville on his original route to link up with Forrest in defense of Selma.

Croxton, meanwhile, regrouping and traveling some 40 miles north of Tuscaloosa through the wilderness, crossed the Black Warrior River near Johnson's Ferry the morning of April 2. From there they marched into Tuscaloosa via Northport down the old Watermelon Road, arriving on the evening of April 3 and capturing Tuscaloosa the following day.

Croxton's force, from the time it left Elyton March 29, 1865 to its arrival in Carrollton, Georgia on April 25, had marched 653 miles in a fast-moving sweep which destroyed five iron-works — including Tannehill — three factories, numerous mills and quantities of supplies.[106] He also took 300 prisoners.

With the works at Tannehill out of commission, Croxton then directed his attention on Tuscaloosa itself. There his men burned a hat factory, nitre works, a shoe factory, the Sipsey Cotton Mills and the Leach and Avery Foundry which is reported to have manufactured Confederate cannon. The biggest target, however, was the University of Alabama where all but three buildings were burned. Among those going up in flame was the university library which contained more than 7,000 volumes.

The university was targeted for destruction because it was thought to be a training ground for Confederate officers. Indeed, its 300 cadets were a part of Tuscaloosa's defense force. There was little opposition to Croxton's movement toward Tuscaloosa although a small skirmish did take place on the covered bridge that connected Northport to Tuscaloosa.

Croxton had planned to rejoin the main body of Wilson's troops in Selma on April 2 but, hearing that Confederates stood in his way, returned to Elyton. Later he marched across central Alabama by way of Trussville, Talladega and Jacksonville and from there went to Macon, Georgia where he joined again with Wilson on May 1, 1865.

Forrest, whose headquarters had been in West Point, Mississippi, attempted to block the federal thrust toward Selma with 3,000 men but the size of his troops prevented any major confrontation. Instead he engaged Wilson in hit-and-run operations between Montevallo and Selma.

When Selma fell on April 2, the Confederacy lost what its military commanders had said was "the most important point in Alabama to defend."[107]

Unlike the troops he commanded in the Tannehill attack, Sutherland was not an Iowan but came from Ohio where he joined the Second Ohio Volunteers as a private in Company C in April of 1861. Rising in ranks as a lieutenant and then as a captain, he became Croxton's assistant adjutant general during the Alabama campaign March 18, 1864, two weeks before the furnaces were hit.[108]

A major figure in Croxton's maneuverings, Sutherland was ordered a few days later after the capture of Tuscaloosa to take a diversionary force (a company of the Sixth Kentucky) toward Columbus, Mississippi to give the impression the Union force was heading in that direction instead of Croxton's actual route toward Demopolis. At Carrollton, Sutherland burned the Pickens County Courthouse. Unable to rejoin Croxton, Sutherland, hotly pursued by Confederates, galloped 120 miles north to Decatur which he reached on April 12.

Of Sutherland, Croxton wrote in his final report May 20, 1865 that he and several other key officers deserved the gratitude of the military "for their hearty and earnest . . . and valuable services so cheerfully rendered . . . throughout the long and arduous campaign."[109]

Sutherland was mustered out of Union service as a major December 18, 1865 and later served two years as a regular army officer in the 17th U.S. Infantry.

As Wilson moved on to Georgia, hostilities in Alabama shifted downstate where Mobile fell before some 47,000 troops under Union Generals Frederick Steele and E.R.S. Canby on April 12, the last major city in the Confederacy to do so.

Within a month from the time Tannehill fell before Croxton's raid, the Confederate Army and the government itself belonged to the same history as the old furnaces.

ORIGINAL ROUTE, Eastern Valley Road as it appears just west of Tannehill Historical State Park. Gen. Croxton had described the hilly red clay road as "all but impassable."

TWO VIEWS, TANNEHILL NOS. 2 and 3 — Both taken from real angles, top photo also shows reconstructed charging bridge running to Tannehill No. 1. Solidified iron rests in the furnace bottoms from the day they were attacked by Union raiders. (George Flemming)

AFTER THE CIVIL WAR, the old furnaces at Tannehill became a favorite place for afternoon outings. Note air pipe and gears in the area where Sanders' old steam engine was located near Furnace No. 3. (From the Harper Collection, Samford University Library)

CHAPTER V

THOUGHTS OF REBUILDING FALL SHORT

"Destroying the usefulness of the great stone furnaces, they left them standing as solemn witnesses to the general destruction. Tannehill was never again to function as a producing furnace."

> — Milo B. Howard
> (Tannehill Furnace and the Confederacy, 1977)

While any plans Alexander had for rebuilding Tannehill after the war were not a part of written history, they apparently attracted the attention of others who shared his dream that the old ironworks might again come alive.

On August 10-11, 1865 Josiah Gorgas, former chief of ordnance for the Confederacy, visited Tannehill to ponder the possibilities.

As ordnance chief, he had first-hand knowledge of Alabama's now defunct iron industry and the potential it held for redevelopment.

Gorgas, son-in-law of former Alabama Gov. John Gayle, had made up his mind to ply the iron trade, a business he noted in his diary, "I have more heart for than any other I have tho't of." His search for a managerial association or employment would take him to Tannehill, Shelby and Brierfield in hopes of getting into the iron business somewhere in Alabama.

At Tannehill, Gorgas stayed with B. J. Jordan, an ironmaster from Virginia who, along with his wife, was "just eking out a livelihood out of the cupola furnace until something better turns up."[110]

"This property consists of three wretched looking furnaces, 6,000 acres of land, excellent ore beds, some good coal lands, and a small water power, capable of driving one small furnace. A tram gently graded runs from the furnaces to the ore bed. It will be valuable when railroads are opened."[111]

Gorgas spent two days at Tannehill looking over ore lands and surveying the area. The Tannehill ore bed he described "as a very fine one, brown hematite in exhaustless quality."

In his entry on August 11, Gorgas states he "rode to the deposits of coal and to the proposed site of a rolling mill on nearby Shades Creek but summarily concluded: "there is not enough water."

HISTORIC TANNEHILL was also a favorite spot for hunters around the turn of the century. William Marion Hamaker (1841-1912) and his wife Sara Jane (Fuller) Hamaker (1859-1939) are shown in this early photo. Mr. Hamaker reportedly once worked at the Tannehill Ironworks. (Iron and Steel Museum of Alabama)

Gorgas moved on to Shelby and eventually Brierfield where, with the help of Francis Strother Lyon of Demopolis, he purchased the Bibb plant as war contraband for $45,000 on January 9, 1866.[112]

Encountering difficulty making the Brierfield operation profitable Gorgas left in 1869 for a position at the University of the South at Sewanee, Tennessee. He would later become president of the University of Alabama.

In 1868, a year before Gorgas left for Tennessee, the old Tannehill site was sold to David Thomas, whose family put together the Pioneer Mining and Manufacturing Company which later would become Republic Steel Corporation.[113]

Republic continued to mine the old Goethite site through World War II as did United States Steel.

Several years after Alexander decided not to reinvest in a new works in Tannehill, prospects brightened for a modern plant at the place. Giles Edwards, an ironmaster in his own right, had set up residence in the "old mansion house" near the Tannehill Furnaces from which he surveyed properties for the Pioneer Company.

Armes relates stories of how Edwards entertained many visitors from Pennsylvania — including members of the Thomas Family — in the "big house" which stood for many years as a Roupes Valley landmark.

On one such occasion, an E. Wilbur from Bethlehem, Pennsylvania inquired about the cost of constructing a modern plant at the old Tannehill site, to which Edwards replied by letter, May 26, 1871:

"1. The cost of building a charcoal blast furnaces at this place, of the following dimensions: Height, 35 feet; diameter at the boshes, nine feet, with hot blast and blowing engine, steam boilers, etc., would be $32,000; a furnace of the above dimensions will make 10 tons of pig iron per day . . .

2. The cost of making hot blast charcoal iron will range from $17.50 to $20.00 per ton.

3. The cost of transportation of pig iron to Mobile from the (nearby) Brierfield Ironworks, the highest rate that I have known was $7 per ton, by rail of Selma and Meridian, Mississippi to Mobile, and from there by sea to New York at the rate of $3 per ton — consult the map and compare the distance from this place — Tannehill and Mobile and Montevallo and Mobile.

4. As to the probable time it would take to build up and get into blast after first breaking ground, I will say that if a start be made the first of August, I believe that I could make about 600 tons of pig iron inside of 12 months.

"Any other information upon this subject that you desire I shall be glad to give at any time."[114]

Wilbur apparently decided against rebuilding at Tannehill and Edwards moved to Woodstock, some eight miles distant, where he began construction of his own blast furnace in Bibb County in 1873. After a

THIS RARE PHOTOGRAPH, probably taken in the late 1890s, shows all
three Tannehill furnaces still standing including remnants of the old
steam engine installed by Sanders in 1863. Note the 16-foot flywheel in
right foreground. (Birmingham Public Library)

redesign of the works and with added funding, the plant was finally blown in 1880 and captured a footnote in history as being the first Alabama furnace to be blown in on coke.[115]

Edwards had worked in the mills of Pennsylvania as a young man before accepting a position at the Bluff Furnace (East Tennessee) in Chattanooga in 1859 which he rebuilt to accept coke instead of charcoal, the first such furnace in Tennessee. When the furnace closed a year later, a portion of the machinery was shipped by Edwards to the new Oxford Furnace near Anniston as has been mentioned in a previous chapter.

During the Civil War, Edwards had served as assistant general superintendent of the Shelby Ironworks which fell to Wilson's raiders in 1865. Shelby also experimented with coke during Edward's tenure.

Shortly after the war Edwards persuaded his old friend, David Thomas of Pennsylvania, to purchase coal and iron ore land in Alabama. Edwards was familiar with the Alabama iron industry and had great faith in its future development, despite the setbacks of war time destruction.

At Thomas' direction, Edwards made a number of land purchases including the old Tannehill site and the surrounding Goethite mines. On December 30, 1868 the Pioneer Company was formed with David and John Thomas and Edwards among its organizers.[116]

Beginning in 1888 the company put into blast the first of the big Thomas Furnaces, followed by No. 2 in 1890 and — under supervision of the Republic Iron and Steel Company — No. 3 in 1903. In April, 1930 all properties of the Republic Iron and Steel Company were taken over by the Republic Steel Corporation which made iron at the Birmingham site until 1973.

The Tannehill site was looked at a third time as location for a possible new iron plant. Daniel Augustus Tompkins, a leading North Carolina industrialist, visited Tannehill in 1881 with the idea of going into business here.

He had made a number of visits to the Birmingham area in the interests of Robert Heysham, an official of the Bethlehem Iron Works in Pennsylvania where, at the time, Tompkins was employed. Obviously impressed with what he saw at Tannehill, he wrote his fiancee, Miss Harriet Brigham, on April 6, 1881, that "the more I think of it the better seems the idea of a plantation in Alabama."

"It would require hard work for some time to pay for it but after all the life would be pleasant, I think. Some people here own a place called Tannehill near to Birmingham with a railroad . . . and much iron ore on it for which they want $12,000. My idea is to try to get (it) from them on time. I could raise enough money to work it myself."[117]

Tompkins was obviously interested in the property for more than agricultural uses. He graduated from Rensselaer Polytechnic Institute in 1873 and served as a machinist and draftsman at the Bethlehem Iron Works from 1874-1881.

REAR VIEW OF OLD TANNEHILL IRONWORKS with Tannehill No. 1 (Single Furnace, 1859) in foreground, probably taken around 1895. Note chimney draft stacks still remain on Tannehill Nos. 2 and 3. (Birmingham Public Library)

While he may have eyed a redevelopment of the iron industry at Tannehill, Tompkins failed to make the move and instead became associated with a glass manufacturer in Missouri. Tompkins then moved to Charlotte, North Carolina in 1883 where he would later become publisher of *The Charlotte Observer.*

The Tannehill site may have been looked at a fourth time as an industrial site but this, too, never materialized. When the DeBardeleben Coal and Iron Company was incorporated in 1886, Col. H. F. DeBardeleben, along with David Roberts and Andrew Adger, planned to build a group of new iron furnaces and looked around for the best possible location.

The plan was to build a new city near Birmingham, the heart of which would be eight furnaces and a steel mill served by at least two railroads. The site selected was in the vicinity of old Jonesboro, 13 miles southwest of Birmingham. They named the new town "Bessemer"[118] after Sir Henry Bessemer, inventor of the steelmaking process that was revolutionizing the industry. His "Bessemer Converter" forced air under pressure through molton pig iron thereby eliminating many impurities.

Here DeBardeleben found all the necessary raw materials for making iron and land he could purchase for $1 an acre. "After months of prospecting and of thought, deliberation and traveling and inspection for miles and miles around and wearing out several fox-trotting horses going from Tannehill to Rising Fawn, Georgia, I could not but feel that here was the opportunity for industries and manufactories of many and various kinds," said DeBardeleben. Bessemer, just 12 miles from Tannehill, was officially incorporated January 6, 1887.

Five blast furnaces would be built in Bessemer including Bessemer Nos. 1 and 2 which went into blast in 1888 and 1889, the Robertstown Furnace, Nos. 3 and 4 and Little Bell Furnace, which all became operational in 1890.[119]

On June 1, 1892 the Tennessee Coal and Iron and Railroad Company purchased the DeBardeleben properties and in this manner the holdings eventually became a part of the United States Steel Corporation.

With Edwards moved from the old Tannehill "mansion house" and with no further plans made to re-open the old furnaces, the land reverted to its natural state.

Other than brown ore and coal mining operations in the area, the historic old Tannehill property was relegated to timber and recreational uses. Several small farms sprang up in the area. Children in the Bucksville area used Roupes Creek, also called Mill Creek and Mud Creek, as a swimming hole and their parents frequently held family outings here.

The old works still exist much the way Wilson's Raiders left them, never having been rebuilt or modernized. With their wooden superstructures burnt during Sutherland's attack, the huge stone furnaces stood alone for over a century as silent sentinels of an industrial age come and gone.

THESE PHOTOS, taken by U. K. Roberts in 1941, show while a great deal of the old furnace machinery had been removed, still much remained including the flywheel and gearing for the steam engine installed in 1863. The big wheel sat in a stone trough, a fourth of it below the ground. (U. K. Roberts)

Restoration of Tannehill No. 1 as a national bicentennial project in 1976 and subsequent work on Furnaces Nos. 2 and 3 begun in 1985 have begun to put the old works back into its war-time appearance. Said Armes in 1910:

> "Old Tannehill is perhaps the most haunting of all the early charcoal furnaces of Alabama. Its ruins still stand in silent watch at the base of a lonely cliff, above Roupes Creek, that slender dark-flowing tributary of Shades Creek. Two massive stacks of solid masonry, builded as the Romans builded 20 centuries ago, great stone on stone — vine veiled — are all that is left today of Moses Stroup's handiwork.
>
> Solemnly the old furnace speaks of the heavy ways of toil long since dead, that our fathers had before us. Majestic in the forest, yet ruling no more, it has a burdened, solitary heart. The very shadows seem to sleep, even as the stones; and the drowsy sun rays circling them are but the brushings of evanescent dreams."[120]

The furnace ruins and adjacent industrial sites remain as a memorial to the early ironmasters, Tannehill being of the first generation of the Alabama iron industry.

A SOLITARY FIGURE walks past Old Tannehill No. 1 in the late 1930s when much of the furnace machinery dating from the Civil War years was still on the ground. (Iron and Steel Museum of Alabama)

THE OLD ALICE FURNACE, Birmingham's first ironmaker, was built in 1880 on First Avenue, North, just west of 14th Street. It made the first basic pig iron in the Birmingham area suitable for open hearth use. This photo from the only print in existence made on the first day of operation. (Birmingham Public Library)

CHAPTER VI

THE RISE OF BIRMINGHAM

"There were developments during the seventies and early eighties that presaged an industrial expansion of which only the most exuberant imagination had dreamed."

— A. B. Moore
(The History of Alabama and Its People, 1927)

While the works at Tannehill would become a part of history, iron making in the Birmingham area would flourish.

The quality of Alabama iron made during the war period had impressed northern capitalists who saw the potential of great return on investment from the state's vast mineral deposits.

The ordnance cast at Selma was most exclusively of Alabama iron. After the war, when the arsenal and the remaining armament were sold as contraband, the big guns were cut up and sent to Philadelphia.[121] Here the quality of the iron attracted the attention of Pennsylvania ironmakers, some of whom had already begun to look for involvement in Alabama prior to the outbreak of hostilities.

The rebuilding of the state's iron industry, however, was not immediate. When the war ended in April of 1865, Alabama entered into a period of stagnation that would run for almost 10 years. With the exception of the Hale and Murdock Furnace in Lamar County, Alabama had lost all its ironmaking capability.

The success of plants at Oxmoor, Irondale and Tannehill had focused attention on Jefferson County and it was here that postwar investors in new ironworks would direct their efforts.

Coming on the heels of incorporation of Birmingham in December of 1871 was the rebuilding of the Oxmoor site in 1872 by Daniel Pratt, Alabama's leading industrialist of the period. He installed his 30-year-old son-in-law, Henry F. DeBardeleben, as manager. Irondale had reopened in late 1865 or early 1866 and for a time, the plant, also known as McElwain Furnace, was the only functioning ironworks in the state when Hale and Murdock shut down in 1870. Iron sold at Irondale for $60 a ton before the furnace was acquired by the Thomas Family of Pennsylvania in 1872.[122]

MARY PRATT FURNACE, the third to be built in Birmingham, went into blast in 1883 along First Avenue, North, between downtown Birmingham and Avondale. Dismantled in 1903. (James F. Sulzby, Jr.)

BESSEMER FURNACES, Nos. 1 and 2, were put into blast in 1888-89, the first of five blast furnaces to be built in Bessemer. Dismantled in 1929, (Bessemer Hall of History)

From 1866 to 1879 Alabama produced less than 30,000 tons of iron annually, all of it except a small amount used by local foundries shipped north of the Ohio River. No. 2 Alabama foundry iron sold for $30 to $48 per gross ton FOB Pittsburgh.[123]

When it was discovered that coke could be made from large nearby deposits of bituminous coal, the rise of Birmingham as a manufacturing center appeared predestined. Beginning with the rebuilding of Oxmoor in 1872, 24 new furnaces would be built in Jefferson County though 1890, in the short period of 18 years.[124]

The original city fathers appeared to be men of unusual vision, an elite group of investors — many Alabama born — who recognized the area's mineral wealth foretold the development of a great industrial center.

From it personal fortunes would be made that would surpass even those of the cotton barons a generation earlier. Among such visionaries was John T. Milner, chief engineer for the South and North Railroad.

From the crest of Red Mountain, Milner would pinpoint the spot where his line would soon be intersected by the east-west tracks of the Alabama and Chattanooga Railroad. Here, he said, would rise a "great workshop town."[125]

Milner's granddaughter later claimed he had a "rather curious and remarkable dream sense" that allowed him to "visualize strangely and see things in the dark."[126] He knew instinctively that land near where the two lines would cross in the vicinity of vast yet untapped mineral deposits could make men of moderate means rich.

Milner's vision was shared by James R. Powell, a Virginian who parlayed a small investment into large land holdings. When the Elyton Land Company was formed to develop the new city, Powell was named president. Much of the funding for the land options, some $200,000, was provided by Josiah Morris, a Montgomery banker who had made his fortune as a cotton broker in New Orleans.[127]

There were others equally as important in the new city's development, the surnames of whom would later find themselves on hospitals, mines and factories, schools and hotels.

They included James Withers Sloss, Benjamin F. Roden, Robert H. Henley, Charles Linn, Frank P. O'Brien and T. T. Hillman, grandson of the builder of the original forge at Tannehill.

The Elyton Land Company offered lots surrounding the proposed rail intersection for $75 to $150 each.[128] Many of those who rushed in to buy lots and build on them did so with the dream that industrialization would make them personal fortunes.

In a short time more than 500 homes and stores were erected along the new town's muddy streets. Birmingham, named for the great manufacturing center of England, was clearly on its way.[129]

Dreams of quick profits, however, were dashed by the Panic of 1873 when the devastating effects of a nationwide depression and a local outbreak of cholera threatened Birmingham's much-heralded development.

The lifting of the depression — some eight years after the first lots for the new city were staked out — now brought northern and English investors in search of a piece of the economic pie Milner had promised would make Alabama the industrial center of the postwar South.

Birmingham's second "boom" period began when investors came to realize good quality pig iron could be made by mixing coking coal with local iron ore. In 1879 the Pratt Coal and Coke Company, owned by Sloss, DeBardeleben and a mining engineer from New York, Truman H. Aldrich, began to supply the area with its first reliable supply of coking coal for this purpose.

That same year construction began on the first furnace ever built in the Birmingham city limits, Alice No. 1. The work of DeBardeleben and Hillman, ground for the historic plant was broken on September 29 along First Avenue, North just west of 14th Street. When it was blown in on November 23, 1880, it became the fourth furnace to be built in Jefferson County. Alice No. 2 went into blast at the same site in 1883.

Alice No. 1 had an average daily output for its first year of operation of 53 tons of foundry iron, a record for the time. Alice No. 2 in 1886 would set a 24-hour production record for the South, 150 tons.[130]

Alice No. 1, also known as "Little Alice," further had the distinction of making the first basic pig iron in the Birmingham district suitable for open hearth use. It played a key role in convincing northern investors that manufacture of good quality iron from coke in Birmingham was practical.

The Linn Ironworks, which originated in 1877 as an iron foundry and finishing operation, was built in part from machinery acquired from the defunct Irondale Furnace which went out of blast in 1873.[131]

Anxious to get on with the industrialization planned for the area, the Elyton Land Company began to practically give building sites away near the railroad junction. The Louisville and Nashville Railroad, which had bought out the ailing South and North line, also granted freight rate concessions.

Ironworks, rolling mills and factories began to spring up in the area which, utilizing easy access to coal, iron ore, rail transportation and cheap labor, produced pig iron at a lower cost than any city in America or England.[132] The mining of bituminous coal climbed even more rapidly.

The existence of bituminous coal was observed in Alabama as early as 1834 by Dr. Alexander Jones of Mobile although little was done to develop the mining of it until after the Civil War.

With the discovery that good quality coking coal for blast furnaces could be found in the Birmingham area, large scale mining operations began in earnest. So extensive were the two Birmingham area fields — the Warrior and the Cahaba — there was no concern of ever exhausting the supply. The Warrior Field is estimated at approximately 9,420 square miles in size, the Cahaba at 360. The Coosa, a part of which is also in Jefferson County, encompasses an area about 210 square miles in size.[133]

ORE WASHER, GOETHITE MINES near Tannehill were operated by the Pioneer Mining and Manufacturing Company to supply the Thomas Furnaces beginning in 1888. Sold to Republic Iron and Steel Company in 1899. (Birmingham Public Library)

THE TANNEHILL NO. 4 WASHER AND TIPPLE in about 1912 after it was purchased by Republic Iron and Steel Company. In both 1909 and 1910, Alabama produced over a million tons of brown ore a year, the Goethite Mines near Tannehill being among the largest. (Geological Survey of Alabama)

Birmingham would rapidly become the center of the most extensive manufacture of coke pig iron in the South. From 1880 to 1883, Alabama more than doubled its annual production.[134]

Equally as impressive to industrial planners were large deposits of iron ore and fluxes (dolomite and limestone). An estimated 4.8 billion tons of red ore underlie areas in Bibb, DeKalb, Etowah, Jefferson and St. Clair Counties. In addition, reserves of brown ore in the southeastern, northwestern and central counties are estimated at about 726 million tons.[135]

While the Birmingham area has the rather striking advantage that nowhere else in the world do large deposits of all three essentials for ironmaking exist side by side, the iron content of the ore is not as high as in some other areas. Ore in the Misabi Range of Minnesota near Lake Superior, for instance, has an iron analysis of 90%. Typical analysis of hard Alabama red ore (hematite) is 37%. Soft red ore, produced when nature's solvent action reduces its limestone content, has an analysis of 50.8%.[136]

Deposits of brown ore (limonite) occur in many locations in the state, the largest in Jefferson, Tuscaloosa and Franklin Counties. Whereas red ore is found in seams, brown ore occurs in pockets. Typical analysis of Alabama brown ore, similar to what is found in the Goethite deposit near Tannehill, runs about 50% iron content.[137]

Given Alabama's great undeveloped mineral wealth, it was not surprising Jefferson County and a number of other localities around the state would be the beneficiary of post-war industrial growth.

Among them were Anniston, Gadsden and Sheffield. Other mining and industrial endeavors were launched in Bibb, Shelby, Talladega and Cherokee Counties. Within the mineral areas of the state, a great boom was underway.

Following Birmingham's example, new cities were created from cow pastures, cotton fields and woodland. Among them was Bessemer, whose planners had dreams it might one day overtake Birmingham as the state's industrial center.

Indeed, in just two years, five furnaces were built in Bessemer with DeBardeleben consolidating his holdings here into the DeBardeleben Coal and Iron Company in 1889.

About the same time, Enoch Ensley, a rich Tennessee planter from Memphis, vowed to build a town of his own, also in Jefferson County, that would surpass Bessemer. To be known as "Ensley," he hoped it would become "the great industrial city of the nation."[138]

Ensley had bought the Pratt Company from the DeBardeleben interest in 1881 when the colonel mistakenly thought he had contracted tuberculosis. It was the first million dollar deal in the history of Birmingham and probably the entire South.[139]

To these holdings, which included vast acreage of mineral lands and beehive coke oven, Ensley added the Alice Furnace and the Linn Iron Company in 1884.

THE OXMOOR FURNACES, located between present day Homewood and Shannon, were acquired by the Tennessee Coal and Iron Company in 1892 after having undergone several expansions and management changes from their rebirth after the Civil War in 1873. The last iron to be made here was in 1928, ten years after this photo was taken by TCI. (George Gordon Crawford Papers, Samford University Library)

LONG BATTERIES OF "BEEHIVE COKE OVENS" were operated by TCI at the old Blocton coal mines near Tannehill in Bibb County, before development of more efficient coke processing with chemical recovery equipment. In 1901, more than 900 men worked at TCI's five furnaces and 720 coke ovens, 1200 more in its rolling mills and pipe plants. (U.S. Steel Corp.)

Two years later Ensley, still building his personal fortune, agreed to sell an option on the Pratt Company to Hillman and Col. Alfred Shook. Hillman had lost control of the Alice Furnace when he sold it to Ensley. Hillman and Shook then resold their option to the Tennessee Coal, Iron and Railroad Company.

Ensley remained as president of the new combined operation which by now — excluding properties in Tennessee — totaled 76,000 acres in coal lands, 460 coke ovens, two blast furnaces and 13,000 acres atop Red Mountain extending some seven and a half miles down the crest.[140]

The Tennessee Company, which would become known simply as TCI, had established itself as the giant of Birmingham iron and steel concerns.

When the Alice Furnace was acquired by TCI, Hillman was made vice president, a position he held until 1889. He later rejoined TCI in 1891 from which position he built the first four TCI furnaces at Ensley. At the time of his death in 1905 he was president of the Pratt Consolidated Coal Company.[141]

The four new Ensley furnaces were capable of producing 200 tons of iron a day each. To these properties, TCI also added 1,400 coke ovens and opened four new coal mines.[142] (A portion of the huge rock abutments of TCI's old Blocton coke ovens was used in the restoration of Tannehill Furnaces Nos. 2 and 3, their size and shape being similar to the fractured original stones.)

The Tennessee Company, which at this time was shipping huge amounts of rail, had gained a preeminent position in Alabama iron making and was, for the first time, competing with the older established iron and steel centers of the north and midwest.

With the acquisition of numerous other properties including the DeBardeleben Coal and Iron Company, TCI by 1900 had put together a giant corporation whose holdings included 13 furnaces, all supplied by its own coal mines, and 400,000 acres of coal and iron ore.[143]

Toward the end of the century as the demand in the metals industry began to shift to steel, Birmingham was faced with an adapt or die situation.

TCI iron already was being used as a source material by steelmakers in other parts of the country, and when the Henderson Iron and Manufacturing Company made the first steel in Birmingham on an experimental basis in 1888, TCI made the decision to begin mass production of it in the Birmingham market.

The following year the company took the necessary steps to enter this new field and created the Alabama Steel and Shipbuilding Company as a subsidiary to operate a steel plant. Construction began on a mill capable of producing 1,000 tons a day in Ensley near TCI's iron plant.

The mill was ready for operation in the fall of 1899 and the first heat of steel was tapped on Thanksgiving Day of that year.[144]

THE EARLY CENTER of TCI's industrial base in Alabama, the six
Ensley Furnaces by 1902 were producing rails from open hearth steel.
More than 400,000 tons of finished steel products were made here in 1906.
(Birmingham Public Library)

While TCI would continue to expand, the Panic of 1907 sent the company into a tailspin as ready credit reserves evaporated. That led to acquisition by United States Steel Corporation on November 1 of the same year.

The purchase, approved by President Theodore Roosevelt and the U.S. Supreme Court, brought charges from Congress it violated the Sherman Anti-Trust Act in that U.S. Steel had acquired a monopoly on openhearth production of steel rails not to mention a lock on the nation's iron ore supply while taking over an up and coming competitor.

U.S. Steel, which had originally rejected a proposal to buy TCI, countered that its change of mind represented a public service to prevent the spread of panic which in 1907 was gripping the country.

No matter the motivation, U.S. Steel acquired in the TCI take-over tremendous ore and coal deposits estimated at $1 billion for the sum of only $35,317,632.[145]

While much of Birmingham's early iron and steel development centered around TCI and U.S. Steel, other companies were also active in the city's industrial development.

By 1900 most of Birmingham's small iron companies had been forced by price competition to merge into Sloss-Sheffield Steel and Iron Company, Republic Iron and Steel Company and Woodward Iron Company.

By now the trend begun in 1881 toward absentee ownership of Birmingham's metals industry had become a reality.

The history of Republic Steel's involvement in the Birmingham district is more closely tied to the old Tannehill operation than any of the big four.

Beginning with acquisition of the burnt-out Tannehill furnaces and the nearby Geothite brown ore mines by the Pioneer Mining and Manufacturing Company directly after the Civil War, the seeds for Republic's presence in Alabama were sown.

The Pioneer Company would continue to acquire mining properties in the Birmingham area for two decades before its first furnace stack was constructed.

The Thomas Family of Pennsylvania, which founded the Pioneer Company, did not consider the time right for development of iron manufacturing plants here until Birmingham's boom period of 1887. That's when it purchased the old Hawkins Plantation and began building the town of Thomas, just four miles west of downtown Birmingham.

The land was bought from the Debardeleben and Aldrich interests for $4 an acre.[146] The company's first blast furnace was blown in on the site on May 18, 1888, the second in 1890. All the properties of the Pioneer Company — including Tannehill — were purchased by Republic Iron and Steel Company, headquartered in Pittsburgh, Pennsylvania in October of 1899.

WEIMER ENGINES at Thomas Works. The No. 3 Furnace, blown in during 1902 by Republic Iron and Steel Company, was the largest in the Birmingham district at that time. (Birmingham Public Library)

Just as the sensation created by entry into the Birmingham district by U.S. Steel in 1907, Republic's earlier purchase was the talk of the business world. At the same time Republic also purchased the Birmingham and Alabama Rolling Mills.

Further, Republic's coal properties at Warner and Sayreton were developed and an enormous battery of coke ovens — said to be the largest in the country (900 beehive ovens) — were built. The company then added a third furnace at the Thomas Works which went into blast June 11, 1902. With a daily capacity of 250 tons, it was the first large furnace built in Birmingham.[147]

While Republic never rebuilt the furnaces at Tannehill, there remains today the letters "RISCO" on the back side of Tannehill No. 3, a mark of ownership from an earlier time.

The Woodward Iron Company, which was located just north of Bessemer, was the closest of the big four Birmingham iron producers to the old Tannehill site. The company was organized in the fall of 1881 and its first furnace went into blast August 17, 1883 on the old Jordan Farm 12 miles southwest of Birmingham.[148] The first log schoolhouse in Jefferson County was located on the same property.

Purchased by the Woodward Brothers, W. H. and J. H., about the same time the Thomas Family was acquiring the old Tannehill property, the company added a second furnace in 1887 and a third in 1905.[149] The Woodward operation was viewed as an experiment in efficiency by other ironmen of the day. The plant was the only one in the state that mined its own coal, ore and limestone and hauled them over its own railroad.

Armes says Woodward iron in the late 1880s was produced at a lower cost than anywhere else in the world.

In 1883, Robert P. Porter, editor of the Engineering Supplement to the *London Times,* visited the Birmingham district from which he wrote:

"This region of Alabama is unquestionably the most interesting in the United States with reference to the interests of iron manufacture in this country. It is, in fact, the only place on the American continent where it is possible to make iron in competition with the cheap iron of England. The cheapest place until now on the globe for manufacturing iron is in the Cleveland region, Yorkshire, England. The distance from the coal to the ore averages them a distance of 20 miles, while in Alabama the coal and the ore are in many places within half a mile of each other."[150]

The Sloss-Sheffield operation was the first in the Birmingham district to begin exporting pig iron to foreign countries in significant amounts although Woodward says there are several known cases of iron being shipped to England from Alabama's pioneer furnaces prior to the Civil War.

THE WOODWARD FURNACES, between Birmingham and Bessemer, were the nation's largest independent and completely integrated manufacturer of merchant pig iron at the beginning of World War II. (Iron and Steel Museum of Alabama)

THE SLOSS CITY FURNACES were a Birmingham landmark until they were closed in 1971. Dating to 1881, this photo shows how they appeared opening day. (William H. Brantley, Jr. Collection, Samford University Library)

Next to TCI, Sloss was the second largest producer of iron in the Birmingham area. Formed in 1899 from the consolidation of 13 iron, coal and ore companies — including the old Sloss Iron and Steel Company (1886) — it operated seven blast furnaces and controlled some 65,000 acres of coal lands and 53,000 acres of ore property. Four of the furnaces were in the Birmingham district, three in Sheffield in Colbert County.

By 1901 Alabama was producing more pig iron per year than any state in the nation except Pennsylvania, Ohio and Illinois. The four states together accounted for 80 per cent of American pig iron production at the turn of the century.[151]

By 1920 Alabama would rank seventh in coal production nationally (16,700,000 tons), third in iron ore production (5,894,001 tons), fourth in coke production (4,221,000 tons) and fourth in pig iron manufacture (2,392,962 tons).[152]

Interestingly enough the same ore used by the Confederacy to manufacture iron and war materials at sites like Tannehill and Oxmoor played a large part in furnishing iron and military materials for the United States in World Wars I and II.

The importance of the Birmingham district in iron and steel making reached a peak in the early 1950s. From the end of World War II in 1945 through 1953, more than 30,000 workers were employed in Birmingham-based primary metal industries. That number dropped to 28,000 in 1960, to 27,000 in 1970 and to 20,000 in 1980. Blast furnaces, however, experienced even more dramatic cutbacks dropping from 17,800 workers in 1970 to only 3,100 in 1983.[153]

By the beginning of the 1980s, a downturn in production by U.S. Steel at its Birmingham plants sent shock waves through the Alabama industry. The big facility at Ensley, which had begun a cutback in the 1970s, closed its rail mill in 1981 and the foundry in 1982. The blast furnaces at Ensley had shut down six or seven years earlier.

Relics of the Ensley Works — including the door to Furnace No. 5 (1900) are on display at the Iron and Steel Museum at Tannehill Historical State Park. They also include rail sections from the last heat of steel there.

The giant mill at Fairfield closed in 1982, which along with the Ensley foundry, put 4,500 U.S. Steel employees out of work. The Fairfield Works would remain idle for a year and a half.

The company then built a new seamless pipe mill adjacent to the old plant in Fairfield putting 600 workers back on the payroll late in 1983 and in early 1984 resumed steelmaking and flat roll operations.

The pipe mill, one of the most modern in America, and the furnace operations including three Q-Bop furnaces and one blast furnace brought U.S. Steel's workforce in Birmingham back to 2,400 by December of 1984. In the early 1950s U.S. Steel had employed 25,000 workers in its iron and steel operations, foundries and coal and ore mines.

BATTERY OF FIRST FOUR Ensley Furnaces as they appeared in 1890. Note log cabins of workers in foreground. (Birmingham Public Library)

THE FIVE BLAST FURNACES at Bessemer contributed to Henry DeBardeleben's dream of making similar developments at Birmingham and Ensley "look like small potatoes." Bessemer Nos. 1 and 2 went into blast in 1888-1889. (Birmingham Public Library)

In July of 1985, U.S. Steel announced a further expansion of its Fairfield Works, a new $110 million continuous slab caster and improvements in the hot strip mill making it one of four key U.S. Steel plants where the company has made a long range commitment to make steel.

Republic's Thomas Iron Works closed in October of 1972 although the company continued its coke works (65 ovens) until the summer of 1982. At the time total employment was only about 100, down from more than 1,000 in the 1920s.

Republic sold its Birmingham property to the Ling, Temco and Vought interests (LTV Steel) of Cleveland, Ohio June 30, 1984.

Woodward Iron Company (Mead Corporation) shut down the last of its pig iron furnaces in Birmingham on January 27, 1973. The old Woodward Iron Company Post Office was moved to Tannehill Historical State Park for preservation in 1979.

Sloss-Sheffield, now owned by Jim Walter Corporation, still operated a blast furnace in North Birmingham in 1985 as well as pipe shops there and in Bessemer. The old Sloss City Furnaces (1882; rebuilt 1927), however, closed in June of 1970 and is now a city museum known as Sloss National Historic Landmark.

Total iron and steel employment (primary metals) in the Birmingham area in 1984 had dwindled to 12,000, a far cry from the 32,000 workers on the job in 1952. Only five companies were still engaged in iron and steel production in the Birmingham district in 1985, U.S. Steel, American Cast Iron Pipe, U. S. Pipe/Jim Walter Resources, Birmingham Steel and Southern Metal Industries.

RAY FARABEE, professor emeritus of chemical and metallurgical engineering at the University of Alabama, served as furnace master for the bicentennial re-fire at Tannehill, September 19, 1976.

CHAPTER VII

TANNEHILL, A NEW BEGINNING

". . . the roots of the New South lay deep in the old but beyond a doubt times had changed."

— John D. Hicks
(The American Nation, 1955)

While many early day Birmingham area ironworks went out of existence, some almost without a trace, a few have remained intact long enough to be noted for their historical significance.

Such is the case with Old Tannehill. Lying dormant for decades, the old forge and furnace site were reclaimed by the wilderness. When Wilson's raiders left the place a smoky ruin in 1865, Ethel Armes says "the whole country round about was abandoned and the forest left to its own."

The "virgin wilderness" Miss Armes described in 1910 became a favorite location for weekend picnics, baptisms and outdoor outings during the first part of the century. Hunting was also popular in the area. The old furnaces built by Stroup and Sanders, she said, stood in the overgrowth like "some castled fortress in Arthurian legend, all over-wrought with briers and lacing vines and ferns."

"Sun light and shadows play hide and seek. The leaves are thick. The openings into the crucibles are arches, cathedral-like, pure gothic in form, full of grace and dark with mystery. A tall sycamore leans its white branches over the ruined stones. A pine tree, 30 feet in height, springs from the mossy top where it is a very jungle of weeds and wild flowers, all growing 40 feet in mid-air. Sumac, sweet gum and the wild muscadine creep close in from the stream that drove the great wheels of Tannehill years ago."[154]

Eyewitness accounts describe a great deal of machinery, pieces of broken gearing, blast engines, wheels and air pipes, scattered about the furnace yard up until World War II. Much of the historic iron mill artifacts were then used as scrap for Republic's Thomas Works. Iron scavenging probably had been going on even years before, some probably sold as scrap to TCI.

Republic Steel guards stationed at the Tannehill property from time to time caught scavengers and made them unload their illegal cargo where they were stopped.

LARGE IRON POT uncovered February 7, 1956 by University of Alabama archaelogical dig near east corner of Single Furnace. Workers may have used the pot for cooling laddles and tongs after making a run of iron. Note the chipped edge which indicates they hit the edge to get crust or slag off their tools. (University of Alabama)

PIPE TRENCH uncovered by UA investigators February 23, 1956 during Tannehill study. Pipe, 10 to 12 inches in diameter in eight-foot sections, carried air from blower house to forge operations on nearby hillside. (University of Alabama)

As late as 1940, U. K. Roberts says, a big metal plate that had supported the brick stack on the Double Furnace was still in place. Area residents, he adds, however, had taken most of the brick away for their own use by 1900.

Roberts, who first began visiting the old furnace yard in the early 1930s, says almost all the old machinery and heavy metal fragments had disappeared by 1944, much of it sold for scrap iron which was selling at the time for $35 to $40 a ton.

A retired U.S. Steel employee who worked in its Wenonah ore processing plant, Roberts recalls seeing an iron bench in front of the Single Furnace along with gears and shafts. A huge fly wheel and some large gearing connected with the old steam engine installed by Sanders in 1863, he says, was the last to go. Two men were arrested and sent to the Tuscaloosa County Jail in 1951 for attempting to carry off the last remaining pieces of the old steam engine including its boiler. They were apprehended when their truck mired down in the roadway just west of the present day museum site.[155] "I would say that vandals and the people who took rock and brick did more damage to the furnaces than did the Yankees," Roberts adds.[156]

Sometime during the early 1920s a discernable crack developed in the front exterior wall of Furnaces Nos. 2 and 3 (Double Furnaces) causing concern on the part of Republic Steel officials that someone might be hurt by falling stone and the company held liable. As a precautionary move around 1925 the company set off several small charges which brought the entire furnace front down, a condition in which the Double Furnace remained until the state began restoration work in 1986.

That there were a great many machine parts and relics around the furnace site is certain. Republic Steel listed 77 — including an air compressor, a stand for shafting, crank arms, an air dome, a water wheel and shaft, a furnace stove and a nail machine — in a memo dated June 18, 1926.[157] The pieces, on which "R. I. & S. CO." was painted in white, were kept by Republic for some time but a hand written note at the bottom of the memo reads "scraped by Republic at a later date."

The University of Alabama also uncovered a great collection of furnace relics in its archaeological investigation in January of 1956. Most of these are now located at the Iron and Steel Museum at Tannehill. They include a large Pitman rod, several large kettles, iron floor plates, cast iron pipes, machine parts, several casting boxes and a large number of metal fragments.

Under a $1,000 grant from the John Alcide and Delia Truss Roberts Charitable Trust a number of additional furnace relics were retrieved from Roupes Creek in the immediate vicinity of the plant site in November, 1985 by the Foundation for Historical Research and Reclamation. These included a 10-foot-long building column and a two-inch air pipe, 6'10" with 7¼ inch flanges on both ends. They are now a part of the Tannehill Ironworks collection at the Iron and Steel Museum at Tannehill.

WALTER B. JONES   **THOMAS DeJARNETTE, JR.**

FRED MAXWELL   **HILL FERGUSON**

NORTHEAST CORNER OF BLOWER HOUSE — A wooden flume to an overshot wheel was located at the camera position, running to the center tier where the wheel turned. (University of Alabama)

OLD FORGE SITE — University of Alabama archaeologists dug this three-foot trench January 20, 1956 just south of the Single Furnace (Tannehill No. 1). The trench was excavated in three-inch levels with a tremendous amount of iron and casting pieces found. (University of Alabama)

Despite the ruinous state of the Double Furnace, which is undergoing restoration, Tannehill No. 1 is one of the best preserved pre-Civil War ironworks in the state. Republic Steel, seeking to have the site protected, donated the old iron plant and 56 acres surrounding it to the University of Alabama in 1952 with the provision a road be constructed and the ironworks be restored or stabilized.

Tuscaloosa County agreed to build the road "of good gravel or chirt surface" into the Tannehill property and promised that if the area were developed into a public park or recreational area it would consider paving it.[158]

The University accepted Republic's offer and appointed an eight-man committee including Dr. Walter B. Jones, the state geologist, and Thomas H. DeJarnette, Jr., head of the University's Moundville project, to prepare a preservation plan.

Others on the committee included Hill Ferguson, Fred Maxwell, Prof. E. C. Wright, Hugh Pallaster, Prof. James Faircloth and Dr. Stewart J. Lloyd.[159]

The committee visited the site in February, 1953 and determined as a first step a topographical map of the furnace area should be prepared followed by an archaeological investigation to pinpoint the exact locations of structures vital to the ironworks operation.

Although some time passed before further action was taken, the committee asked the University for $3,500 for architectural designs, blueprints and archaeological studies on August 29, 1955, which amount was approved. Dr. Jones proposed the archaeological study, which was to take 30 days, begin as soon as possible.[160]

Excavations began January 17, 1956 in what had been thought to be an old nail factory. Centrally located in the structure was what appeared to be the remains of a forge. Further investigation, however, revealed it to have been a two-room building with a fire place in each room, probably an office or dwelling. The "forge" was actually a large double hearth, chimney brick from which was scattered about the area.

Excavation of material found at 10 inches below the surface revealed a large amount of slag, indicating the area was at one time filled. Some window weights and seven nails, from one to three inches long of the old square type, were also found.

Remnants of the old blower house located between Furnace No. 1 and Roupes Creek could be clearly seen even before the excavating began. Removal of dirt from the interior revealed this structure to have two outer walls and an inner wall extending some five feet below the surface and resting on a stone floor.

Immediately atop the floor was found a quantity of charred wood and a large number of wrought iron nails. This indicated that the blower house, built on top of the stone walls, had burned and dropped to the lower level, apparently a victim of Wilson's Civil War Raid.

Among objects recovered were a large gear about 10 inches in diameter, a large u-shaped bearing housing and a Pittman rod six feet long and three inches in diameter.

DAMAGE BY VANDALS — This is how Tannehill No. 1 (1859) appeared from 1968 to 1975 after unknown persons blew out a corner section with dynamite before the property was given state protection. The damage cost thousands of dollars to repair.

The structure is thought to have supported a water wheel connected by a shaft to a bellows-type apparatus as the air supply for Tannehill No. 1, built 1859 and perhaps for an earlier forge or bloomery operation. Remains of a dam across the creek are also in evidence from which a race and wooden flume brought water to the wheel.

The blower or mill house and the two-room building originally believed to have been the nail factory both were burned.

Digs just south of the Single Furnace revealed the remains of an old forge thought to have dated to Hillman's and Tannehill's operations. Large quantities of cast iron material were uncovered at this location as well as a wooden ductway lying two feet below the surface which may have been used to carry air to the old forge on the nearby hillside.

Also located close by was the old foundry site. Stone foundations were uncovered which would indicate a structure approximately 28 by 32 feet. Large slabs of cast iron were found placed horizontally on the floor indicating at least part of it was covered. A large cast iron pot was found about three inches below the surface embedded in the floor, probably used as a receptacle for tongs used in handling ladles for hot metal. The rim area of the pot nearest the furnace had been worn completely away indicating workers had hit the edge to get the slag off their tools.[161]

The University ended its excavations at Tannehill March 20, 1956 and all relics uncovered were housed at Smith Hall on the university campus for a number of years. They are now a part of the collection of the Iron and Steel Museum at Tannehill.

While the University contemplated using the Tannehill site as a geological station or survey camp, it was also interested in persuading the State Department of Conservation to develop a state park at the site.

Fred Maxwell, Jr., consulting engineer for the University and a member of the Tannehill archaeological committee, wrote Earl Mc-Gowin, director of the Conservation Department in Montgomery on July 6, 1951, urging him to act favorably on the suggestion.

"If I am successful in obtaining the road to this site and the University comes into possession of the land, will your Department be in the position to (act) favorable toward some development of this park to make it available to, and attractive for the general public?" he wrote. "There is a fine creek near the furnace and the nature of the land lends itself well for development into a public park."[162]

McGowin responded that while he thought the idea of developing the old Tannehill site into a public park was a good one, unfortunately his department had no funds for such a project.

Neither did the university. Most of its money going into preservation work was committed to the old Indian restorations at Moundville.

On March 17, 1967, Ed Lewis, lieutenant governor of the Alabama Central District, Civitan International, wrote University of Alabama President Frank A. Rose urging him to get behind the state park idea.

"We have long hoped that we could do something to develop this area as a state park," Rose responded on April 26, "but at the present time we are trying to develop another project, Moundville Park."

Rose said the Legislature had appropriated only $60,000 a year to the Indian preservation work at Moundville and that he would hesitate to seek additional funding for Tannehill while that work proceeded.

Another prime mover of the park idea was Hill Ferguson, chairman of the Board of Equalization in Jefferson County and, like Maxwell, a member of the archaeological study committee. Ferguson thought the furnace site should be preserved as a monument and the area surrounding it made into a public park.

Nothing, however, would happen at Tannehill in a development sense for the next dozen years although various local groups — including Civitan Clubs at Woodstock and Tuscaloosa — repeatedly called for some government protection for the area. Committees were formed and legislators contacted. The idea for a state park at the site was again suggested to the Conservation Department and its new head, Claude Kelley. The request was again denied.

Then late in 1968 vandals — perhaps in an attempt to discourage the state park idea — dynamited a section of the Single Furnace. Rumors had it that a whiskey still was located in the area. Although no one was ever prosecuted for the wanton destruction, the action refueled efforts to get the Legislature to protect the Tannehill area as a state property.

Due primarily to the efforts of Sens. E. W. Skidmore of Tuscaloosa and Eddie Hubert Gilmore of Bessemer, the Alabama Legislature declared the site a state memorial park commemorating Alabama's iron and steel industry on October 2, 1969 and created the Tannehill Furnace & Foundry Commission as a state agency to administer the preservation activity.

In adopting Act No. 994, legislators created a 16-member board with one member each appointed by the University of Alabama Board of Trustees and the Alabama Historical Commission and the rest by the governor.

The commission was charged by the Legislature to "preserve, restore, maintain and promote as a state park or historic site the land and relics of the Tannehill Furnaces and, in recognition of the important part played by the iron and steel industry in the development of the state, to exhibit this old furnace as an example of the process of making iron in this state's early days."[163]

A. B. Schwarzkopf, then plant manager of United States Pipe & Foundry's Bessemer plant, was named the commission's first chairman. Dan Kilgo, a Tuscaloosa advertising executive, served as its first vice chairman.

Other original appointees included S. E. Belcher, Jr., Jim Bennett, Tunstall R. Gray, Dorothy Henry, Ed Lewis, Sam Maury, Jim Oakley, Sr., W. L. Russell, Margaret Sizemore, R. E. Smith, H. A. Snow and J. Dudley West, all named by Gov. Albert Brewer.

The University of Alabama selected Dr. Walter B. Jones, who had been a member of its Tannehill archaeological study group in 1956, and the Alabama Historical Commission named Dr. Charles G. Summersell, a noted Alabama historian and professor of history at the University of Alabama.

SEN. E. W. SKIDMORE

SEN. EDDIE HUBERT GILMORE

AL SCHWARZKOPF

DAN KILGO

Belcher was in the lumber business; Bennett a newspaper reporter; Gray, of Woodward Iron Co.; Mrs. Henry was associated with the camping community; Lewis, a member of the Woodstock Civitan Club which promoted the park idea; Maury, an attorney with U.S. Steel; Oakley, publisher of the *Centreville Press;* Russell, a parts distributor in nearby Bucksville; Mrs. Sizemore, dean of women at Samford University; Smith, president of Local 1013, United Steelworkers of America; Snow, Jefferson County engineer; and West, an official of Republic Steel.

Ed Nelson, manager of Holiday Beach (Resort) near Woodstock, and a member of the Woodstock Civitans, was selected as the park superintendent. Early in 1970 more than 300 Boy Scouts from the Bessemer District cleared away acres of overgrowth and trash in the area of and approaches to the ironworks site as part of the national Boy Scout "Save Our American Resources" Program (SOAR). Soon thereafter the first building, an old peanut house dating to the 1890s, was moved into the park from the farm of Sen. H. P. James near Sprott in Perry County. It currently serves as a country store and houses administrative offices.

To meet public demand, Tannehill State Park facilities grew by leaps and bounds over the next 15 years spreading across 1,000 acres in Tuscaloosa, Jefferson and Bibb Counties.

A number of historic structures were moved into the park to replace those Sutherland destroyed in 1865 or which had been torn down over the years, beginning with the Stamps Cabin (Perry County, 1870) and the Marchant House (Tuscaloosa County, 1871), both in 1971. The following year the Dunkin House (Perry County, 1871), Stewart House (Bibb County, 1877) and the Hogan House (Bibb County, 1834) were added.

All were original pioneer log cabins of varying designs. The Stewart House had been the residence of the late State Rep. N. E. Stewart. Also in 1972, the old Kimbrell Methodist Church (1905), vacant for 15 years, was moved to the park from its original location northeast on Eastern Valley Road through gifts from many of its former members.

Four more old log homes were acquired in 1974 including the Crocker House (Jefferson County, 1884) and the Bagley House (Jefferson County, 1856), the Thompson House (Bibb County, 1835) and the Snead House (Bibb County, 1850).

Three of the houses were built by Confederate soldiers, the Snead by Col. Henley Graham Snead, commander of the 44th Alabama Volunteers; the Thompson by Samuel Thompson, who was captured at the Battle of Lookout Mountain in 1863 and died a prisoner of war at Rock Island, Illinois in 1864; and the Bagley by John Bagley, who died in a military hospital in Chattanooga, Tennessee of pneumonia and is buried in the Chattanooga National Military Cemetery.

In 1974-75 work began on Tannehill Farm including relocation of the Williams House (Bibb County, 1889) and various out-buildings taken from the George Stewart Farm (Bibb County, circa 1870s). The oldest

OLD TAPAWINGO BRIDGE — This rare iron truss bridge (1902) was relocated near Hall's Gristmill at Tannehill by Jefferson County in 1975. It formerly spanned Turkey Creek near Pinson in the area where the Jefferson County militia drilled prior to the Civil War.

THE IRON AND STEEL MUSEUM of Alabama at Tannehill houses one of the most complete collections of early ironmaking machinery and products in the South, including many relics of the Tannehill Furnaces. It opened in 1981.

structure in the farm complex is a milk storage building dating to 1822 which was moved from the Bolling Farm near Maplesville in Chilton County in 1976.

The farm exhibits the most extensive collection of early day farm machinery in the state, a gift of Dr. H. C. Springer of Bessemer. Also located at this site is a blacksmith shop, sorghum mill, gear shed, various old barns and a smoke house.

As work progressed on the farm complex, a complete re-build of the John Wesley Hall Gristmill and Cotton Gin was begun under a grant from the Linn-Henley Charitable Trust in 1975. The original mill, which operated on the banks of Cooley Creek from 1867 to 1931, replaced an even earlier mill burned by Union troops in the Tannehill raid a mile to the west on Mud Creek. The two bodies of water, all spring fed, converge in the park to form Roupes Creek above the furnace site. The rebuild of the gristmill was patterned after the Reconstruction era mill and opened to the public in 1977.

The 1867 mill is thought to have been built by Col. Tannehill, who although in his seventies at the time, desired to get back into business after the Civil War. Before Tannehill died at age 79 in 1875, he sold his interest to Hall.

The 1870 Agricultural and Manufacturing Census lists Ninian Tannehill as owner of the mill which had a daily grinding capacity of 60 bushels and a capital investment of $1,500. Powered by a water wheel, it employed one person full-time at an annual salary of $200 and in 1870 operated year around. The manufacturing census indicates the mill was a large one and ground both wheat and corn into flour and corn meal.[164]

Col. Tannehill is buried along with his wife, Mary Polly Prude Tannehill, in the old pioneer cemetery at Bucksville. She died in 1882. Although perhaps best known as a farmer and stock raiser in his early days, Tannehill had a keen interest in industrial undertakings as evidenced by his iron plant and gristmill.

It is not clear what his involvement might have been in the original gristmill that operated on Mud Creek near the furnace. That facility was operated by John Kimbrell whose brother, Thomas, was employed at the Tannehill Furnaces.[165] It is a certainty Col. Tannehill was familiar with the nearby gristmill operation and probably learned gristmilling as an observer. The site of the original gristmill has been identified at Tannehill Historical State Park along the old trail that ran from the furnaces north to Eastern Valley Road.

The nearby community of Kimbrell was named for the Kimbrell brothers who moved to Roupes Valley at an early date.

In 1975 Jefferson County relocated the old Tapawingo Bridge (1902) over Cooley Creek near the restored gristmill. The span, over which thousands of Birmingham residents crossed Turkey Creek in the early 1900s, is an excellent example of an early iron truss bridge. Tapawingo, located near Pinson, was a favorite swimming hole and resort area at the turn of the century along the old Blountsville Road.

TANNEHILL SCENES — (top) Kimbrell Methodist Church (1905); Old Dairy Barn (1822), oldest building at Tannehill; (middle) John Wesley Hall Gristmill, a replica of an 1867 mill, constructed on site in 1975-76; (bottom) Woodward Iron Company Post Office (1914) and the Furnace Masters Inn (1976).

In 1976 the park built the Furnace Masters Inn as a country restaurant patterning its construction after the log recreational hall at Judson College at Marion. The University of Alabama donated the logs for the two-story structure.

Two units of the E. W. Skidmore Learning Center, a joint project of the University of Alabama and the Tannehill Furnace & Foundry Commission, were brought into the park in 1978-79. They included the Fowler House (1860), relocated from near West Blocton in Bibb County for use as a converted country school, and the old Woodward Iron Company Post Office (1914) for use as a materials center and administrative office. The Cane Creek School (1923), originally located near Warrior, was added to the complex in 1983. It was the successor to one of the first schools ever built in Jefferson County on land donated by William Thomas in 1815.

The Nail House (Jefferson County, 1860) and the Hosmer House (Tuscaloosa County, 1911) were moved into the park in 1984. The Nail House was built by Jules Nail near Mt. Olive a year before he joined the Union Army.

In a major expansion funded by the Legislature in 1981, the Iron and Steel Museum of Alabama was added as a repository of early day iron products and production equipment as well as relics from the Tannehill Ironworks. The museum, which also includes the Walter B. Jones Center for Industrial Archaeology, traces Tannehill history from the days of the Creek Indians, who lived along the banks of Roupes Creek, through the coming of the iron industry and the Civil War.

The Belcher House (Bibb County, 1870), and the Collins House (Lamar County, 1870) and the Wendell Stewart House (Bibb County, cir. 1855) were relocated in 1985 as was the Peel House (Shelby County, 1890).

Averaging a quarter million visitors a year by the mid-1980s, Tannehill had become one of Alabama's best attended tourist attractions. As a bicentennial project in 1976 (Tannehill was designated an Alabama Bicentennial Park) Tannehill Furnace No. 1 was put back into blast on September 16 for an actual run of iron. By September 19 more than two and a half tons of pig iron had been extracted from the works, most of which went into casting several full-sized Confederate style field cannon and souvenir ingots.

The Smithsonian Institution said it marked the first time in American history that an iron furnace, out of blast for over a century, had ever been put back into operation.[166]

U.S. Steel contributed 50 tons of iron ore for the re-run, 20 tons of limestone and 150 tons of coke. American Cast Iron and Pipe Company donated an industrial blower to provide the needed air power and Abex Corporation lent technical assistance and protective equipment.

More than 50 volunteers from a half dozen Birmingham area steel companies including U.S. Steel, Woodward Iron Company, Abex Railroad Products, Koppers Company, Pullman-Standard, Stubbs Foundry and American Cast Iron and Pipe Company joined the effort.[167]

A TURNOUT ESTIMATED at 15,000 was on hand for the refiring of Tannehill No. 1 as a national bicentennial project September 19, 1976. It marked the first time a Civil War period ironworks had ever been put back into blast after being dormant for over a century. (Birmingham Post-Herald)

MORE THAN 30 iron, steel and metallurgical supply companies either sent volunteer workers or equipment to be used in the Tannehill refire including U.S. Steel, Woodward Iron and Republic Steel Corp. (Birmingham Post-Herald)

SOME TWO AND A HALF tons of pig iron were extracted from the Tannehill bicentennial run in 1976 from a furnace temperature placed by an optical pyrometer at 3100°F. (Raymond Moore)

Furnace master for the historic run was Ray L. Farabee, professor emeritus of chemical and metallurgical engineering and foundry teacher at the University of Alabama. *The Tuscaloosa News* estimated more than 15,000 people watched the final day's tapping.[168]

Making the event possible was restoration work earlier in 1976 to repair the hole in the south furnace wall done by vandals in the dynamiting in 1968, rebuilding the overhead charging bridge burned during the Civil War, relining the furnace core and rebuilding the brick draft stack.

The park commission committed $127,000 to the project bringing together funds from the State of Alabama, the U.S. Department of Interior, the American Revolution Bicentennial Administration, the Alabama Historical Commission and Birmingham area locals of the United Steelworkers of America, AFL-CIO.

The park, using legislative appropriations, committed another $111,000 to begin restoration of Furnaces Nos. 2 and 3 (Double Furnace) in 1985. Talk of restoring the furnaces for a run of iron actually began as early as 1952. The suggestion was included in a letter of December 4, 1952 from Walter B. Jones, the state geologist, to Fred Maxwell, consulting engineer for the University of Alabama.

"You are certainly correct that the single stack should be completely restored. The restoration should include making a run of pig iron. The double furnace should be restored except for operating machinery. I do not believe it would be sound practice to have a lot of rubble at any restoration . . ."[169]

The Tannehill Furnace restoration marks the largest scale rehabilitation of a pioneer iron works since the Saugus Furnace project in Massachusetts was completed in the 1950s. The Saugus plant (circa 1650), the first successful integrated ironworks in America,[170] was restored with funding from the steel industry.

Ironically, the 17th Century plant in Massachusetts and the 19th Century works at Tannehill were similar in design indicating little in the way of ironmaking furnace improvements had been made in 200 years. Truncated furnaces of the Saugus and Tannehill types were of basic design dating to Roman times. Both were charcoal furnaces and both used sand molds. As might be expected, Tannehill No. 1 was somewhat bigger, 30 feet high compared to about 21 for Saugus. Saugus was capable of producing about eight tons of pig iron a week, Tannehill No. 1 about five or six tons a day.

A comparison of the iron content done by *Modern Castings Magazine* in 1970 also shows some similarities:

Chemical composition of Saugus Furnace metal.

Element	Percent
Carbon	2.92
Silicon	1.40
Sulfur	0.060
Phosphorus	0.866

Manganese	0.03
Chromium	0.08
Nickel	0.05
Copper	Trace
Molybdenum	Trace
Vanadium	Trace
Tungsten	Trace
Tin	Trace
Aluminum	Trace
Carbon Equivalent	3.60

Chemical composition of Tannehill Furnace casting.

Element	Percent
Carbon	3.12
Silicon	1.173
Sulfur	0.192
Phosphorus	1.192
Manganese	0.48
Aluminum	0.02
Arsenic	0.023
Chromium	0.02
Copper	0.02
Antimony	0.001
Molybdenum	0.002
Nickel	0.02
Titanium	0.02
Vanadium	0.01
Tin	0.007
Lead	0.002
Carbon Equivalent	3.96

The higher sulfur content of the Tannehill iron may indicate use of coal mixed with charcoal.[171]

Indeed, coal almost completely replaced charcoal as a fuel source in Birmingham area furnaces beginning in 1877. The works at Tannehill may have pointed the way to a number of innovations. The mining of brown ore at the nearby Goethite deposit which began in 1830 was the first evidence on record of strip mining in Alabama.[172] When Moses Stroup built the first of the three blast furnaces at Tannehill in the late 1850s he experimented with red ore from Red Mountain marking the first time Red Mountain iron ore was used.[173] It would later become the area's main ore supply and far outstrip brown ore in local pig iron production.

From Hillman's 1830 forge to the bigger Civil War-era blast furnaces of Stroup and Sanders, Old Tannehill gave first light to Birmingham's iron and steel industry that a century later glowed red in the evening sky.

TANNEHILL NO. 1 with casting shed shortly before historic refire in September, 1976. Looking on is Ed Nelson, superintendent, Tannehill Historical State Park.

THE THREE HUGE BLAST FURNACES at U.S. Steel's Fairfield Works had a rated capacity of over 4,000 tons a day in 1960. Along with its 12 open hearth furnaces, Fairfield was producing almost 4 million tons annually that year. (U.S. Steel Corp.)

PIPE MILL — Shown here prior to completion, the Fairfield pipe mill buildings cover 20 acres. In the background are the blast furnaces and coke plant of Fairfield Works. (U.S. Steel Corp.)

THE NO. 8 BLAST FURNACE at Fairfield can produce 5,000 tons of pig iron a day. Today it's one of the most modern in the South. (U.S. Steel Corp.)

EPILOGUE

Although the Alabama iron industry is usually associated with Birmingham and the huge amounts of raw material needed for making iron in the immediate area, the real pioneers of the industry were the old charcoal furnaces in the wooded hills of surrounding counties.

Ironmaking in Alabama, which dates from 1815 when Joseph Heslip put the Cedar Creek Furnace into blast near Russellville, was born in small stone iron plants using charcoal and brown ore mostly in rural areas of counties like Tuscaloosa, Bibb, Shelby and Talladega.

Of the 15 iron plants (20 furnaces) in blast in Alabama during the Civil War, only two were located in Jefferson County, Oxmoor and Irondale. At Confederate urging, they were added in 1863 to help bolster the South's sagging iron supply.

A single blast furnace at U.S. Steel's Fairfield Works, using imported high grade red ore instead of brown and coke instead of charcoal, turns out more pig iron in one day than most of the old Alabama furnaces could manage in a year.

By comparison, Fairfield No. 8 (1978) has the capability of producing 5,000 tons of pig iron per day, Tannehill No. 1 (1859) five or six tons. The increased production, coming from size and vastly improved technology, in no way belittles the smaller furnaces of a century earlier. Theirs was a vital first step that led to the development of Birmingham beginning in 1871 as one of the nation's largest manufacturers of pig iron. Today it remains as the South's most heavily industrialized city.

Improvements in the Alabama iron industry in the 100-year span from 1860 to 1960 were remarkable.

In 1860, the state had only six blast furnaces . . . Cane Creek (Calhoun County), Little Cahaba No. 1 (Bibb County), Shelby No. 1 (Shelby County), Round Mountain (Cherokee County), Hale & Murdock (Lamar County) and Tannehill No. 1 (Tuscaloosa County) with a total capital investment of $225,000. They produced about 12 per cent of the total iron product in the South and less than 1 per cent of the nation's.

In terms of tonnage Alabama furnaces in 1860 turned out 1,742 tons, 5 per cent of the South's total and under .1 per cent of the national figure.[174]

Before the Civil War came to a close in 1865, however, Alabama was producing more iron for the Confederacy than all other Confederate states combined.[175]

A hundred years later capital investment in Alabama iron and steel manufacturing including rolling and finishing mills had risen to $30 million in 14 plants, 11 of which were in Jefferson County.[176]

Somewhat ironically Alabama's newly emerging iron industry at the time of the Civil War led to its invasion by Union forces. Realizing the importance of Alabama pig iron production to the South — and the huge ordnance works at Selma — Maj. Gen. George H. Thomas, commander, Department of the Cumberland, U.S. Army, ordered its destruction.

Marching on direct orders from Thomas, Maj. Gen. James H. Wilson, 12,500 cavalrymen and 1,500 dismounted men of the Division of the Mississippi, launched such a massive sweep through the state on March 22, 1865 that the end of the first week in April would see every iron plant in Alabama razed — except one, the Hale & Murdock Furnace in Lamar County.

Out of the way and not along Wilson's lightning-like offensive from Lauderdale County through Elyton, Selma and Montgomery, the plant continued to operate until five years after the war's end.

The furnaces at Tannehill were hit by a detachment of Wilson's cavalry on March 31, 1865 while Furnaces Nos. 2 and 3 were still in blast. Their solidified iron mass yet remains in the furnace bottoms.

Although the damage caused by the Union raids was considerable, it did not in itself cripple the Alabama iron industry. On hit-and-destroy missions, Yankee cavalry had neither the time nor the means to dismantle the huge stone and brick furnaces. They did, however, burn all the adjacent factory buildings made of wood and charcoal supplies and destroy the usefulness of essential equipment including steam engines, blowers, mill houses, casting fixtures and boilers.

Already the technology of the Civil War-era iron plants was becoming outdated. Coal and coke were replacing charcoal as fuel and iron shell furnaces were considered superior to the old stone-jacketed facilities of Roman design.

Even if the war had not laid them in ruin, the Alabama furnaces of 1865 were due for major technological overhauls. That would come 10-15 years later. For eight years after the war's end, the Alabama iron industry was almost dormant. Then, in a single year, four new furnaces were built, all of more modern design and with northern capital.

In an unprecedented expansion of the industry from 1880 to 1900, some 42 new blast furnaces were erected in the state beginning with construction of the Alice Furnace in Birmingham by Col. H. F. DeBardeleben on First Avenue, North just west of 14th Street. Put into blast in November of 1880, Alice No. 1 was the first ironworks built within the Birmingham city limits. The stack measured 63' x 15' and its daily output averaged in the first year of operation 53 tons — a record for the time.[177]

With the addition of the new furnaces iron production in Alabama rose from 69,000 tons in 1880 to 1,185,000 tons in 1900. That figure increased to 2,392,962 tons in 1920 and four million tons in 1950. In that year Alabama ranked first in the nation in grey iron castings, third in iron ore production, seventh in coal mining and sixth in pig iron production.[178]

While many of the furnaces of the earlier part of the century were built on the original locations of even earlier ones, six of Alabama's old Civil War-era plants would never be put back into blast as producing iron mills including the furnaces at Tannehill, Little Cahaba, Knight and Cane Creek.

Tannehill No. 1, however, was restored and put back into blast for a run of iron as part of the nation's bicentennial celebration on September 16-19, 1976.

Considering the technological changes that took place after the Civil War in iron manufacturing in the South, the war might well have been a mercy killing for the old charcoal furnaces. Somewhat ironically, Tannehill, as a tourist attraction, may have attracted greater economic importance than it had as an iron producer. With more than a quarter million tourists a year, a third of them from out-of-state, the historic site adds thousands of dollars a year to the Greater Birmingham economy.

Without the rich history of the old ironworks, however, the park would not hold its unique attraction. The furnaces at Tannehill were a pacesetter for the larger plants to follow. Its early experiments with coke and hot blast equipment pointed the way to an improved technology the South had for too long ignored. It, along with its sister plants at Oxmoor, Irondale and Brierfield, would bridge one era to another, a giving away of an outdated manufacturing process to a more modern one the North had already adopted.

The legacy of the old mills, as well as those that were modernized and given new life, provided a vital beginning for Alabama's iron and steel industry which would make the state the South's leader in manufacturing, products of which today are shipped around the world.

END OF A MOUNTAIN — This cut along the entrance road to Tannehill Historical State Park marks the western terminus of Red Mountain. (George Flemming)

APPENDIX I

GEOLOGY OF THE OLD TANNEHILL FURNACE SITE

(Roupes Valley Iron Works, Sanders Furnaces)

As reported in the University of Alabama's archaeological excavation of the furnace site, January 17-March 20, 1956.

Location

The old Tannehill Furnace Site, the sixth oldest blast furnace site in Alabama, is situated in the extreme east central part of Tuscaloosa County near the Bibb and Jefferson County lines. The 55.3 acreas of the area cover all of the Southeast ¼ of the Southwest ¼ of Section 33, Township 20 South, Range 5 West and parts of the adjoining Southwest ¼, the Northwest ¼, and the Northeast ¼ of the Southwest ¼ of Section 33.

Physiography

The furnace area lies along the southeastern fringe of the Birmingham - Big Canoe Valley in the Valley and Ridge Province of the Appalachian Highlands. A prominent northeast - southwest sandstone ridge parallel to and southeast of Red Mountain and a sandstone ridge to the southeast of this first-mentioned sandstone ridge form the local valley in which the old blast furnaces are nestled. Mud Creek (Tannehill Mill Creek) flows southeast and curves to the southwest past the furnace site. The highest and lowest elevation are 540 feet and 420 feet respectively above mean sea level.

General Geology

The Floyd shale of Mississippian Age underlies the entire area of the furnace site. This shale with its accompanying Hartselle sandstone has been folded and forms the southeastern flank of an eroded anticline (Red Mountain) whose axis strikes about N30°E and dips uniformly about 35°SE.

Southeast of the furnace site across Mud Creek the Parkwood sandstone caps the ridge which forms the southeast boundary of the site. A two-foot bed of ferruginous, fossiliferous limestone containing Archimedes fossils underlies this Parkwood sandstone and is thought to be part of the Floyd shale formation.

Slickensiding parallel to the bedding of the Hartselle sandstone indicates some faulting in the area, but no movement was measured.

Of particular interest in the vicinity of Old Tannehill Furnace are the Paleozoic rocks outcropping along the road to the furnace area. A general cross-section from west to east from where the first road turns off the county road at Tannehill to the furnace site shows the Copper Ridge and Ketona cherty dolomites, the Chickamauga limestone, Red Mountain formation, Chattanooga shale, Fort Payne cherty limestone, Floyd shale, and Parkwood formation which outcrops just east of the furnace area.

---

* Geology taken from Burchard, Ernest F. and Butts, Charles, *Iron Ores, Fuels and Fluxes of the Birmingham District, Alabama,* U. S. G. S. Bulletin 400, 1910; in conjunction with field work by Earl L. Hastings, Geological Survey of Alabama, under the supervision of Hugh D. Pallister, Geological Survey of Alabama, in cooperation with the Alabama Museum of Natural History and the University of Alabama.

APPENDIX II

From Confederate Records, Rebel Archives, War Department, CSA Imprint (William Stanley Hoole Special Collections Library, University of Alabama).

NOTE: The contract for pig iron between the Confederacy and the William L. Sanders Iron Works (Roupes Valley Iron Works) was attached to a report from John C. Breckinridge, Secretary of War, to Jefferson Davis on the status of Southern iron works and forges in 1864 requested by the Confederate House of Representatives February 14, 1865.

CONTRACT FOR PIG IRON, WITH W. L. SANDERS

This contract, made this 23rd day of March A.D. 1863 between W. L. Sanders of the first part, and the Confederate States of America, through I. M. St. John, Lieutenant Colonel and Chief of the Nitre and Mining Bureau, of the second part, witnesseth, that in consideration of the conditions herein after named, the party of the first part covenants and agrees to manufacture and deliver on the cars of the Alabama and Tennessee River Rail Road, at Montevallo, 4,000 tons of pig iron per annum, of which not more than 15 per cent, shall be in No. 3 hot or cold blast iron; not more than 35 per cent, in No. 2 hot or cold blast iron; and the balance to be in No. 1 hot or cold blast iron.

The delivery to commence within 10 days after the contract shall have been duly executed, and to be made in nearly equal quarterly installments: the delivery in no one month, however, to fall below 150 tons.

As there is a haul of 18 miles from the works of the party of the first part to the point of delivery, and the roads are liable to be so much·broken up by bad weather, so that the party of the first part may not be able to deliver the full amount of 1,000 tons per quarter, it is agreed that any excess of iron delivered in any other quarter shall be credited to the quarter in which he may be deficient: Provided, that in no event he shall fall below the amount stipulated to be delivered per annum.

The iron thus delivered is to be subject to inspection by an officer of the Nitre and Mining Bureau, or an authorized agent thereof, and to be by him weighed and classified as to the quality and grade; according to which payments are to be made. All pig metal shall bear the initials, and the name of the furnace marked upon the pig.

In consideration whereof, the party of the second part agrees to pay to the party of the first part, his agents or assigns, after inspection, proof and approval of said iron, the following prices, subject to modification and reduction, as herein after provided, to wit:

For No. 1 charcoal cold blast pig iron, per ton of 2,240 (lbs) $75.00
For No. 2 charcoal cold blast pig iron, per ton of 2,240 (lbs) 67.50
For No. 3 charcoal cold blast pig iron, per ton of 2,240 (lbs) 62.50

For No. 1 charcoal hot blast pig iron, per ton of 2,240 (lbs) 65.00
For No. 2 charcoal hot blast pig iron, per ton of 2,240 (lbs) 55.00
For No. 3 charcoal hot blast pig iron, per ton of 2,240 (lbs) 50.00

All payments for iron delivered shall be made once in each month. The parties hereto mutually reserve the right, during the existing war with the United States, to modify these prices so as to preserve the same relation between the price of the iron and the cost of the articles necessary to its production, as is established in the above recited scale; and in order to make such modifications with justice to both parties, it is agreed that during the war, when either party shall so desire, a board of assessment be convened to review the above scale of prices: Provided, however, That no such board shall without mutual consent, be convened prior to the month of January 1864, or more frequently thereafter than once in year. Said board shall be composed of one member, chosen by the party of the first part; of a second, chosen by the party of the second part; and in case of disagreement of these two, of a third, to be chosen by them: and in lieu of the prices above enumerated, the prices assessed by the board for the different grades of iron, shall be paid by the party of the second part until modified by the subsequent board, or reduced as herein provided, by the establishment of peace relations with the United States. Such reduction shall not begin until six months after the close of the existing war: Provided, That the price of provisions, labor and forage on the 1st day of January 1863 shall be the basis upon which such modification of prices shall be made.

The original scale of prices above written, subject to the following modification, shall then rule and control the compensation of the party of the first part, viz: 80 per cent of the above written prices for the ensuing six months; 60 per cent, thereof for the then next ensuing six months; and 50 per cent, thereof until the 1st day of January 1867, when the contract shall expire.

It is expressly agreed by the parties to this instrument, that a reservation of 10 per cent will be made upon all payments during the first year, and the same per cent for each subsequent year until the termination of this contract, to reimburse the party of the second part for any advance made to the party of the first part; which reservation or deduction shall be accredited yearly as a reimbursing fund upon the advance made: Provided, That said reservation or deduction of 10 per cent on gross amount due for iron delivered, shall be sufficient to repay such advance by the 1st day of January 1867. Should it not be sufficient, then a larger per cent shall be deducted; which per cent shall be fixed on the 1st day of January of each year for the ensuing 12 months, taking the deliveries of the previous year and the length of time this contract has to run before its termination, as the basis on which such increased deduction shall be made.

It is further agreed by the parties, that any excess in the quantity of pig iron herein named, which the party of the first part may be able to produce in any year during the continuance of this contract, shall be the property of the government, and will be received and paid for at the prices herein before provided in this contract: Provided, That it shall be at the opinion of the party of the second part to receive such excess: and in case they do not require such excess, then the party of the second part shall give to the party of the first part a notice of 30 days; that after the expiration of said time they will only receive the amount of iron stipulated in this contract as absolute delivery.

To enable the party of the first part to finish the furnace now under construction, it is agreed that the party of the second part shall advance to the party of the first part $50,000 in bonds on the Confederate States of America — one-half on the signing and ratification of this contract; one-fourth on the requisition of the party of the first part; and the remaining one-fourth, upon a second requisition of the party of the first part; said requisitions to be accompanied by a certificate of an inspecting officer (specially appointed), that the antecedent installments have been judiciously expended for machinery, labor, materials and fixtures essential for the production of the iron hereby contracted for: and to enable the inspecting officer to give such certificate, full information and access to the books of the party of the first part shall be given to the inspecting officer.

It is further agreed, that satisfactory security, in twice the sum of the advance so made, shall be given by the party of the first part to the party of the second part, for the return of the money so advanced, with interest at the rate of eight per cent per annum, if the advances are made in treasury notes; but if the advances be made in bonds, then the same rate of interest as the bonds bear.

To insure the fulfillment on this contract, it is agreed that the party of the second part shall reserve 10 per cent on all payments due for iron delivered under this contract until its completion. This reservation of 10 per cent shall be refunded to the party of the first part, upon a yearly settlement to be had when a balance of interest shall be struck, provided it shall appear that the party of the first part has complied with the provisions of this contract. And it is further expressly provided, that should the party of the first part willfully refuse to make the deliveries to the party of the second part, as slated, or deliver iron to other parties (except by order of a duly authorized agent), or make other disposition of it than provided for in this contract with the Confederate States, or for any other purpose than executing this contract, as above stated, or shall fail to refund the said advances according to the terms and stipulations of this contract, the party of the second part shall have the right to enter into and take possession of the said iron works of the party of the first part, including all the lands, houses, furnaces, tenements, wagons, teams, tools, &c., and other things thereto belonging, to enable the party of the second part to work the said iron works on their own account, during the existence of this contract; but the exercise of this right by the said Confederate States of America shall not be held or regarded to be a release or extinguishment of the claim of said Confederate States of America for any balance which may be then due by the party of the first part, on account of advances heretofore reserved by them; but the said party of the first part shall be entitled to a credit from said Confederate States of America, during their possession of said property, taken and used as aforesaid, of the annual value of their property; said value to be assessed each year by a board of arbitrators, one of whom shall be selected by each party, and these two to select a third: Provided, however, That should it happen at any time that cars cannot be procured, by reasonable diligence on the part of the party of the first part, for the purpose of delivery, then and in that event, the failure to deliver on the cars shall not be considered a forfeiture of this contract; but the party of the first part is authorized, in the event cars cannot be procured by reasonable diligence, or in the event they are not furnished by the rail road, or by the party of the second part, to store or deposit the iron at or near the point of delivery: Provided, That a seizure of the works of the party of the first part shall be made only after a full investigation of the alleged defalcation of the party of the first part, by an agent duly appointed by the party of the second part, and after a hearing of the defense of the party of the first part.

The party of the second part reserves the right to decide all questions arising under this contract, and to judge of the execution thereof, and also the right to declare the same forfeit, should there be no delivery of iron within 10 days from the date hereof; or if at any time hereafter the party of the first part shall fail or refuse to comply with the covenants and agreements herein made.

All payments on account of this contract will be made, when the iron is received and accepted, in treasury notes.

Executed in duplicate, the day and year first above written, by the signature and seal of the said W. L. Sanders, and for and in behalf of the said Confederate States of America, by the signature and seal of I. M. St. John, Lieutenant Colonel and Chief of the Nitre and Mining Bureau aforesaid.

Signed, sealed and delivered
    in the presence of

V. B. Waddell,   WILLIAM L. SANDERS. (Seal.)
J. F. Sellers,

H. F. Reardon, as to   I. M. ST. JOHN. (Seal.)
                                              Lt. Col. & Ch'f Bur.

Whereas W. L. Sanders did, on the 23rd day of March 1863, enter into a contract with the Confederate States of America, through Col. I. M. St. John, for the manufacture of pig iron.

Now, in accordance with said contract, we do hereby appoint A. C. Wurzbach to act for the Confederate States, and D. H. Kenney to act for W. L. Sanders, to assess the prices of pig iron from the first of July 1863; which prices are to be fixed until another board of commissioners shall be appointed. Should these two above named commissioners disagree, they shall select an umpire.

                          (Signed) I. M. ST. JOHN.
                                   Lt. Col. & Ch'f Bur.

                          (Signed) WM. L. SANDERS.

                                —

                                              Selma, July 1st, 1863

We, the board of commissioners appointed for the purpose of reviewing the prices of pig iron, and assessing them anew to correspond with the prices of provisions and labor, do, in accordance with the above instructions, assess, for and in the case of Wm. L. Sanders, that he receive for all pig iron to be manufactured and delivered after the 1st of July, 1863, $100 for No. 1 C. B. (cold blast) pig iron; $90 for C. B. pig iron No. 2; and $75 for C. B. pig iron No. 3.

                          Respectfully submitted.
                          (Signed) A. C. Wurzbach,
                          (Signed) D. H. Kenney,
                                   Board of Commissioners

A similar assessment for 1864 fixes the prices as follows:

For No. 1 pig iron, cold blast ....$160 per ton
For No. 2 pig iron, cold blast ....$144 per ton
For No. 3 pig iron, cold blast ....$118 per ton

APPENDIX III

ROSTER OF UNION TROOPS ENGAGED IN THE ATTACK ON THE TANNEHILL IRONWORKS, MARCH 31, 1865

COMPANY D, EIGHTH IOWA CAVALRY, First Brigade, First Division, United States Cavalry Corps, Military Division of the Mississippi.

Captain - Lovene Hopkins
1st Lieutenant - Jacob D. Hardin
2nd Lieutenant - John C. Power
Officer in charge of detachment to Tannehill - Capt. William A. Sutherland, Asistant Adj. Gen., First Brigade

ENLISTED

Andrews, Henry C.	Hendricks, James K.
Armstrong, James E.	Homewood, Nelson
Atwood, Walter N.	Hoyt, Washington, Jr.
Beals, Silas	Huff, John H.
Bear, John	Hunter, John C.
Benson, James A.	John, Mordecai
Blair, George G.	Keller, Benjamin
Blake, Theodore W.	Kelley, Charles
Brown, Thomas	Kephart, Conrad
Campbell, William H.	Kirkham, Orlando
Christy, William	Kirkham, Rodolphus
Clapp, William L.	Knight, Edward F.
Conley, Elijah	Knight, Washington M.
Conley, William	Lamb, Thomas J.
Cox, Henry C.	Lee, William H.
Crawford, Francis M.	Linton, Edmond
Cusyn, Joseph S.	McClure, Abner L.
Daniels, Jacinth A.	McMannus, Hezekiah
Danner, Samuel A.	McMullen, William A.
Darnold, Thomas N.	Mace, Harrison
Deselm, Lyman F.	Mickey, John H.
Douglass, Martin	Miller, George W.
Downer, Joseph B.	Miller, Joel E.
Ellis, John	Milliner, Andrew T.
Everett, Burrus S.	Millman, Nathan C.
Fitzgerald, Barton L.	Morrison, George M. D.
Fullerton, James R.	Myers, William H.
Gookin, Thomas	Nida, Mathew H.
Graham, Benjamin I.	Nobles, Giles J.
Graham, Lorenzo D.	Norris, Joseph
Gregory, Thomas M.	Park, Asa G.
Hammann, Henry	Power, John C.
Hardin, Jacob D.	Reed, John F.
Harless, Nathaniel	Ross, McKendree
Harper, William E.	Ruby, Addison S.
Hellyer, David	Ruby, Boanerges F.

Rushing, Jesse E.
Scott, James W.
Shey, Thomas
Stark, Samuel H.
Stricklin, Henry
Stults, William H.
Templeton, Wesley G. L.
Thompson, Jesse H.
Tillford, Temolioun W.
Trask, Cornelius B.

Trask, Theodore P.
Turgeon, John
Vance, Robert
Vance, Truman
Walkinshaw, John H.
Weeles, Peter
Williams, Daniel C.
Williams, Samuel H.
Williams, James T.
Wossom, Hiram

COMPANY I, EIGHTH IOWA CAVALRY

Captain - Elliott Shurtz
1st Lieutenant - Harmon A. Jones
2nd Lieutenant - Andrew F. Tipton

ENLISTED

Adams, James A.
Allen, Elias P.
Applegate, William E.
Armstrong, Bennett A.
Arrasmith, James D.
Baker, Charles R.
Ball, Frank
Beaman, Horace S.
Beeson, Wilson B.
Bente, William
Best, Marsee J.
Bitters, Jacob
Brock, Cloud H.
Browne, Thomas
Burdick, Lavern W.
Chandler, Levi
Chiles, William W.
Cleaver, Josiah J.
Coolidge, Henry P.
Cowan, Richard
Cowan, Thomas M.
Crawford, James
Davis, Patrick
Dobson, Stephen N.
Elliott, Jared
Evans, Martin V. B.
Evans, Noah H.
Farguson, Richard
Fitzpatrick, John M.
Fuller, William C.
Gaige, L. S.
Garwood, Cyrus
Godwin, Henry
Godwin, King H.

Green, James A.
Haiden, William
Hall, Alva H.
Hart, John
Hass, Gilbert R.
Hixon, George J.
Holt, William
Hughes, Josiah
Hull, Samuel B.
Hunsdom, Lewis
Johnson, Daniel W.
Knowlton, Charles F.
Krutsinger, Thomas S.
Lane, Gilbert S.
Luke, Isiah
Luke, John
McCain, James M.
Mackey, David H.
Michael, George W. S.
Milholen, Perry
Mitchell, Daniel
Monlux, Ezra
Monlux, George
Monlux, John
Moon, William A.
Morrill, Edward A.
Nichols, Thomas
Nichols, William R.
Noble, Joseph
O'Neil, John
Parman, James W.
Patterson, Melvin A.
Peete, George L.
Peeters, Isaac M.

Pegg, Gamaliel
Pyle, John
Rahe, William
Rathbone, Sylvanus
Ray, Henry
Rice, Alexander
Rickey, Jasper N.
Rowley, Eli
Satterlee, William
Schultz, Charles
Shriner, George
Shurtz, Elliott
Stewart, Thomas
Stickney, John

Stow, Washburn A.
Straight, James S.
Sutton, Barnabus B.
Terrill, Lander C.
Thomas, Francis M.
Thomas, John B.
Thorp, Aaron G.
Tipton, Andrew F.
Vanallen, John
Watrous, George
Welch, John
Williams, George
Windish, Herman
Woods, Daniel W.

Special notes, Company I:
— Corp. Frank Ball was wounded April 6, 1865 in Tuscaloosa; Gilbert R. Hass was wounded April 5, 1865.
— A number of men from this company were taken prisoner in the advance on Atlanta in the fighting at Newnan, Georgia, July 30, 1864.
— George Monlux, who provides an eyewitness account of the burning of the Tannehill Furnaces on March 31, 1865 in his narrative on Wilson's Raid, was 21 at the time the iron works was hit. Monlux was promoted to company commisary sergeant June 1, 1865 and second lieutenant, August, 1865. His last known address was Elkader, Iowa in 1933. See Chapter IV.

Special notes, Company D:
— John H. Huff was promoted to second lieutenant, January 29, 1865.
— Jacob D. Hardin was promoted to captain, July 15, 1864
— John C. Power was promoted to captain, January 29, 1865, resigned March 21, 1865.
— Addison S. Ruby, who is quoted on the campaign at Tuscaloosa in Chapter IV, was 25 when he took part in the attack on Tannehill. At the time of his military retirement he served as 4th sergeant, Company D. His last known address was Indianola, Iowa in 1935.
— Jesse H. Thompson was taken prisoner at Sipsey Springs, Alabama, April 6, 1865.

Note: This roster taken from Roster and Record, Iowa Soldiers in the War of the Rebellion, Vol. IV, State of Iowa, Adjutant General's Office, Des Moines, Iowa, 1910, pp. 1525-1639. (On microfilm, Samford University Library, Birmingham, Alabama.)

APPENDIX IV

RELICS AND HISTORICAL OBJECTS UNCOVERED BY REPUBLIC STEEL CORPORATION AND THE UNIVERSITY OF ALABAMA AT THE OLD TANNEHILL FURNACE SITE IN 1926 AND 1956

Republic Steel Corp. Memo

Rickey, Alabama, June 18, 1926

Following is an inventory of all the remaining old parts at the Old Tannehill Furnace on Mud Creek. The pieces were uncovered and assorted out with an identifying number and "R. I. & S. CO." painted in white on each piece:

Number	Description	Number	Description
1	Support for liners	37	Crank arms for driving
2	Support for liners	38	Crank arms for driving
3	Support for stack	39	Crank arms for driving
4	Support for stack	40	Crank arms for driving
5	Support for liners	41	Drive shaft
6	Liners for stack	42	Fly wheel
7	Liners for stack	43	Drive shaft
8	Support for liners	44	Boxes
9	Liners for stack	45	Door frame - top of furnace
10	Liners for stack	46	One piece air compressor
11	Support for stack	47	Air compressor
12	Support for stack	48	One 90 degree ell
13	Support for stack	49	One square air coupling
14	Liners for stack	50	One piece air compressor
15	Liners for stack	51	One 90 degree ell
16	Two 90 degree ells	52	One piece 8″ pipe
17	One 90 degree ell	53	One piece 4″ pipe
18	Trigger lever	54	One piece circular pipe
19	Trigger lever	55	One piece 2″ pipe
20	Trigger lever	56	One piece circular pipe
21	Liner for stack	57	One air dome
22	One 90 degree ell	58	One 8″ 90 degree ell
23	One piece 12″ pipe	59	One piece T iron
24	One piece 12″ pipe	60	One piece shafting
25	One piece 12″ pipe	61	One piece 2″ pipe
26	Square coupling for air compressor	62	One piece drive arm
27	Square coupling for air compressor	63	One 12″ 90 degree ell
28	One piece 12″ pipe	64	One 12″ 90 degree ell
29	12″ 90 degree ell	65	One piece water wheel and shaft
30	One piece 2″ pipe with two ells	66	One piece 12″ pipe
31	Stand for shafting	67	One piece water wheel and shaft
32	Stand for shafting	68	Two pieces 12″ pipe
33	One piece 12″ pipe	69	One piece furnace stove
34	One spur gear	70	One piece gear
35	One spur gear	71	One piece gear
36	Crank arms for driving	72	One piece gear

Number	Description	Number	Description
73	One piece gear	76	One piece gear
74	One piece 12 × 16 square iron	77	One piece furnace door.
75	One piece nail machine		

Scrapped by Republic Steel at a later date.

- - - - - - - - - - -

University of Alabama Archaeological Investigation, Old Tannehill Furnace Site, January 17, 1956 - March 20, 1956.

Number	Description	Place Located
1	Several pieces, window weights	Office or dwelling
2	Seven nails, square, wrought iron	Office or dwelling
3	Iron plate, 3′ × 4″, tapered	Office or dwelling
4	Several pieces broken skillets, pot legs, old castings	Single furnace area
5	Several pieces, skillet rims, hollowware castings	Single furnace area
6	One piece cast iron pipe	Blower house
7	One gear wheel, 10″ circumference,	Blower house
8	One large "V" casting	Blower house
9	One large U-shaped bearing housing	Blower house
10	One large Pitman rod, 6′ × 3″	Blower house
11	Several large slabs cast iron flooring	Foundry
12	One large iron pot	Foundry
13	One large cast iron pipe elbow connecting to eight foot sections of a cast iron pipe line, probably air supply to forge, 12″ diameter	Forge
14	One large cast iron ell	Forge
15	One section cast iron plate, 3′ square with 2″ hole in center	Forge
16	Assortment, steam engine parts	Steam Engine Site
17	Bottom half, large fly wheel	Steam Engine Site
18	One large verticle shaft, 20″ square	Single Furnace
19	One piece, pig iron, 6″ long	Single Furnace
20	Six lengths, eight′ sections, pipe	Blower house to forge
21	Two iron grates	Forge
22	One large iron plate, 45″ square, 2″ thick, hole in center, 36″ diameter	Forge
23	One gearing housing, old wash tub	Blower House

The university excavation also yielded large amounts of scrap iron, pot handles and legs, broken castings and pipes of various sizes.

Not mentioned in the university's study were a number of items found in the collection including four casting boxes, 16½ × 16½ and a large iron front plate, 8 × 37½, bearing raised lettering as follows: "RVIC & Wm. L. S.", obviously a reference to the Roupes Valley Iron Company and its owner from 1862 to 1865, William L. Sanders. This plate may have been used in the bottom of sand molds for pig iron ingots shipped to the Selma Arsenal in compliance with the Confederate requirement all incoming iron be marked for inspection purposes. (See page 134).

SUBSEQUENT FINDINGS

Foundation for Historical Research and Reclamation Survey of Roupes Creek near the Tannehill Ironworks Site, November 23, 1985.

Number	Description	Place Located
1	Iron beam or building column, 10 feet long	Roupes Creek
2	One piece 2″ pipe, 6′ × 10″ with flanges, each end, 7¼″	Roupes Creek
3	One piece iron, sword-shaped, 18½″	Roupes Creek
4	One piece iron, tong-shaped machine part, 2″ × 1¼″ × 19″	Roupes Creek
5	One cutter gate, 7″ × 3¾″	Roupes Creek
6	One piece iron plate, light, 11¹⁰/₁₆″ × 3⅝″	Roupes Creek
7	One horse shoe	Roupes Creek

Various iron fragments, nails, slag pieces and other small items were also uncovered. The FHR&R study was prompted by the discovery in the same area in August, 1985 of a small three-legged cook pot, 6″ × 8¼″, by a swimmer.

TANNEHILL FOUNDATION

Excavations conducted by the Tannehill Foundation in February and March, 1986 in the old foundry area on the hillside behind Tannehill No. 1 also resulted in significant finds including machine parts, several No. 1 "Bscuit Oven" (sic) lids and a No. 4 Oven measuring 5″ deep by 12″ across.

Studies were made on two sites, one which was obviously a large foundry, the second which appeared either to be a smaller foundry or the cooking area for furnace and foundry workers. The "No. 4 Oven" found near a large hearth at the smaller foundry site was 2½ feet below the surface indicating it may have been positioned on a tripod over a hole in which a fire was built. Burnt wood was found in the hole. More than 300 old square nails were also uncovered in the hearth as well as hinge and gate parts, more than likely having been in waste wood used for fires. The hearth measured 7′ × 7′ from the outside walls.

Since the Confederate contract signed with Sanders March 23, 1863 (See Appendix II) stipulated all the iron from Tannehill was to be shipped to the Selma Arsenal, the finds at the foundry yards may have been from operations prior to that time. Miss Armes, however, in "The Story of Coal and Iron in Alabama" (1910) writes in addition to pig iron, munitions and other castings, the works at Tannehill made "pots, pans and skillets for the use of the Confederate Army" all during the war years. It is uncertain how strictly the Confederate contract was enforced.

EXCAVATIONS IN 1986 uncovered a part of the foundry area behind the Tannehill Ironworks including this hearth (top), measuring 7′ x 7′ and a "No. 4 Oven" (bottom), probably used in cooking for furnace workers.

APPENDIX V

ALABAMA LAW

(Regular Session, 1969)

Act No. 994   S. 748—Skidmore, Gilmore, Morrow, Vacca, Bailes, Hawkins, Dominick, Givhan, McCarley, Childs

AN ACT

Relating to state parks, memorials and historical sites; establishing the Tannehill Furnace and Foundry Commission as a state agency to acquire, renovate, maintain and exhibit the old Tannehill Furnace in the County of Tuscaloosa; and to establish, create, manage, control and operate a state memorial park for the exhibition of this old furnace and the processes of iron making and for other related purposes; prescribing the authority, powers, duties and functions of the commission and its members and officers; forbidding members of the commission or employees thereof to engage in certain dealings with the commission and prescribing penalties therefor; and making an appropriation.

Be It Enacted by the Legislature of Alabama:

Section 1. There is hereby created the Tannehill Furnace and Foundry Commission to establish, operate and maintain as a state park or historic site the land and buildings in the County of Tuscaloosa where one of the State's early ironworks, known as the Tannehill Furnace and Foundry was located. The purpose of the commission shall be to preserve, restore, maintain and promote as a state park or historic site the land and relics of the Tannehill furnace, and, in recognition of the important part played by the iron and steel industry in the development of this state, to exhibit this old furnace as an example of the process of making iron in this State's early days.

Section 2. (a) To this end the commission is authorized to take possession, under a lease or a deed, of the land and other property in the County of Tuscaloosa, known as "Old Tannehill Furnace," which is now owned by the University of Alabama; and the Board of Trustees of the University of Alabama is hereby authorized, in its discretion, to lease or to deed in fee simple such lands and appurtenances thereto to the commission. Such board of trustees may also sell, give, or lend any other relics of old-style iron making or other items appropriate for display along with or as a part of a display or exhibit of iron making. The commission is further authorized to lease, accept as a gift or loan, or otherwise acquire any other property, real or personal, including gifts or bequests or other things of value to be used in fulfilling the purpose for which it is established or for any auxiliary purpose incidental or appropriate thereto.

(b) The commission is also authorized to borrow money and issue revenue bonds in evidence thereof; but no such bonds shall be general obligations of the State of Alabama or any agency or any political subdivision thereof. Nor shall such commission pledge to the payment of any such loans the land, buildings, exhibits or other appurtenances thereto. It may, however, pledge to the repayment thereof the proceeds derived from admission fees or charges or other fees or charges made in connection with such park or historical site.

Section 3. (a) The commission shall operate or provide for the operation of the park or historic site hereby provided for, and any appurtenances thereto in such manner as to facilitate its exhibition to the public either with or without a charge. If the commission, in its discretion, decides that a charge is appropriate then the commission shall fix and provide for the collection of such charge or charges as it deems appropriate for admission to the park and for the use, viewing of or other enjoyment of exhibits and other facilities appurtenant to the park.

(b) The commission may enter into agreements with any civic organization, lay group or industrial, professional or governmental organization relative to the general management of the park or historic site. The commission is also specifically authorized to accept gratuitous services from individuals and organizations, and to employ such hostesses, guards, superintendents and other employees, as in its opinion, are needed for the operation and exhibition of such park or historic site.

Section 4. The commission shall be composed of sixteen members, one of whom shall be appointed by the Board of Trustees of the University of Alabama, one of whom shall be a member of the Alabama Historical Commission, chosen by such commission in the manner prescribed by it, and the remaining fourteen members shall be appointed by the Governor. Four of the first members appointed by the Governor shall be appointed for eight-year terms, four shall be appointed for six-year terms, four shall be appointed for four-year terms and two shall be appointed for two-year terms. The first member appointed by the Board of Trustees of the University and the first member representative of the Alabama Historical Commission shall be appointed for two-year terms. Successors to these first members shall all be appointed for eight-year terms. Vacancies on the board, during a term shall be filed for the unexpired portion of the term in the same manner and by the same appointing authority as the member whose place is being filled.

Section 5. No member of the commission shall receive any pay or emolument other than his actual expenses incurred in the discharge of his duties as a member of the commission. All such expenses shall be paid from the funds of the commission. Further, it shall be unlawful for any member of the commission or any employee thereof to charge, receive, or obtain, either directly or indirectly, any fee, commission, retainer or brokerage out of the funds of the commission, and no member of the commission or officer or employee thereof shall have any interest in any land, materials, or contracts sold to or made or negotiated with the commission, or with any member or employee thereof acting in his capacity as a member of such commission. Violation of any provision of this section shall be a misdemeanor and upon conviction shall be punishable by removal from membership or employment and by a fine of not less than $100 or by imprisonment not to exceed six months, or both.

Section 6. The commission shall be a state agency and shall have exclusive control over the Tannehill Furnace and Foundry and the area appurtenant thereto; the memorial park established hereunder; and all improvements and exhibits located thereon; and any additions constructed, created, leased, acquired or erected in connection therewith.

Section 7. The commission shall hold an annual meeting in the City of Tuscaloosa. Eight members shall constitute a quorum for the transaction of business. Additional meetings may be held at such times and places within the State as may be necessary, desirable or convenient upon call of the chairman, or in the case of his absence or incapacity, of the vice-chairman, or on the call of any three members of the commission. The commission shall determine and establish its own organization and procedure in accordance with the provisions of this Act, and shall have an official seal. The commission shall elect its chairman, its vice-chairman, its secretary and its treasurer, and such officers shall hold office for a period of one year or until a successor is elected. Neither the secretary nor the treasurer need be members of the commission. The commission may require that the treasurer thereof be bonded in an amount to be determined by the commission.

Section 8. The commission shall constitute a body corporate and shall have, in addition to those set forth specifically in this Act, all powers necessary or convenient to effect the purposes for which it has been established under and by the terms of this Act, together with all powers incidental thereto or necessary to the discharge of its said powers and duties.

Section 9. This commission shall have a tax exempt status, and the properties of the commission and the income therefrom, all lease agreements and contracts made by it, all bonds issued by it and the coupons applicable thereto and the income therefrom, and all indentures executed with respect thereto shall be forever exempt from any and all taxation by the State of Alabama and any political subdivision thereof, including, but not limited to, income, admission, amusement, excise and ad valorem taxes.

Section 10. For the purpose of effectuating the provisions of this Act there is hereby appropriated out of the funds in the state treasury not otherwise appropriated the sum of *$10,000.00* dollars for each of the fiscal years ending September 30, 1970 and September 30, 1971. The moneys hereby appropriated shall be released only on order of the Governor.

(D) The governing body of any county or of any municipality in this state shall be authorized, by resolution duly adopted and recorded, to appropriate any available public funds not otherwise pledged to the use of any such Commission.

Section 11. The provisions of this Act are severable. If any part of the Act is declared invalid or unconstitutional, such declaration shall not affect the part which remains.

Section 12. All laws or parts of laws which conflict with this Act are repealed.

Section 13. This Act shall become effective immediately upon its passage and approval by the Governor, or upon its otherwise becoming a law.

Approved September 12, 1969.

Time: 8:00 P.M.

I hereby certify that the foregoing copy of an Act of the Legislature of Alabama has been compared with the enrolled Act and it is a true and correct copy thereof.

Given under my hand this 2nd day of October, 1969.

McDOWELL LEE,
Secretary of Senate.

GLOSSARY OF IRONMAKING
OR MANUFACTURING
TERMS USED IN THIS VOLUME

Beehive coke oven — a structure resembling a beehive in front designed to reduce coal to coke for use as fuel in a blast furnace; lined with refractory brick and charged from the top, also utilizes a spray of water. The coke is removed by tearing out a temporary wall covering an arched front or from a door built for the purpose. Beehive ovens were about 12½ feet in diameter and seven feet high. They were capable of producing about 3.1 tons of coke from five tons of coal.

Bessemer converter — an iron furnace design dating to 1856 which revolutionized the manufacturing of steel; named for Sir Henry Bessemer of England, the process forces air under pressure through molten pig iron eliminating most of the silicon and manganese and all of the carbon by oxidation.

Bituminous coal — a coal of good burning quality representing the fourth stage in the development of the fossil fuel; deep black in color, widely used in producing coke for use in iron furnaces.

Blast — the air forced into the bottom of an iron furnace to augment the combustion of the fuel source, charcoal or coke.

Blast furnace — an ironmaking apparatus using iron ore, fluxes and charcoal or coke in which air, hot or cold, is forced into the bottom. It takes roughly two tons of ore, .9 ton of coke, .4 ton of limestone or dolomite and 3.5 tons of air to produce one ton of pig iron.

Bloom — a semi-finished piece of iron or steel resulting from the forming or rolling of an ingot; sometimes beaten with a hammer to give it strength and shape. Derived from the early English term, bloma, in early days it referred to the lump produced in the bottom of a furnace.

Bloomery — an iron plant which usually used charcoal for fuel and a forced air process powered either by a steam engine or bellows. The last iron produced in America in a bloomery was in 1901. In early terminology, a bloomery was essentially a Catalan forge raised in height to produce more iron.

Blower house — a structure housing the blowing apparatus for an iron furnace, usually a large bellows operating off a water wheel to provide the air supply for an early type furnace.

Bosh — the widest portion of a blast furnace; the inverted frustrum of a cone immediately above the hearth.

Brown ore — limonite, basic iron ore of early Alabama furnaces the iron content of which varies from 52 to 66% iron.

Cast iron — an iron usually used for pots, pipes or heavy casting containing a large amount of carbon; not suitable for fine moldings.

Charcoal — a porous carbon produced from burning wood under controlled conditions, usually in dust pits; used as the primary fuel in early Alabama iron furnaces. Charcoal replaced wood as the fuel source in metal smelting in the Bronze Age.

Coke — a solid, coherent, cellular residue of the destructive distillation of bituminous coal processed by high temperatures, usually in coke or beehive coke ovens; used as a fuel source in blast furnaces replacing charcoal. Well established, especially in northern states during the Civil War, coke furnaces by 1869 out produced charcoal furnaces by 553,341 tons to 392,150. In the next decade coke became the primary fuel source for American iron furnaces.

Cupola — a variety of blast furnace in which the metal and the fuel are in immediate contact, similar to early American furnaces; also refers to the remelting of pig iron and scrap for purposes of making iron suitable for foundry use. A cupola furnace to remelt iron for casting purposes was first used in France in about 1700.

Forebay — a reservoir or canal from which water is taken to run equipment, as a waterwheel or turbine.

Forge — an apparatus, usually made of stone, where iron is reheated and hammered into new shapes; sometimes also refers to a furnace where iron is heated.

Fluxes — basic material added to the charge in an iron furnace to unite with sand, ash and dirt during the melting process to remove impurities; forms slag. Fluxes include dolomite and limestone.

Foundry iron — pig iron graded for foundry use.

Hollowware — iron cast into vessels including bowls, pots and cups that have a significant depth and volume.

In-blast — the charging and firing of an iron furnace for a run of iron, in the beginning and continuously throughout the hot process.

Ingots — elongated blocks of iron made by pouring molten iron into molds, usually of a standard size, for purposes of shipping to finishing mills or ironworking shops. Ingots at Tannehill ranged from 18 to 33 inches long and were about three and a half inches deep; also called pigs.

Ironstone — a synonym for iron ore, used mostly in pioneer times.

Kiln — a heated enclosure or oven for processing a substance such as brick by burning, firing or drying.

Leaches and banks — terms used in the manufacture and storage of gunpowder in a 19th Century nitre works; in the leaching process of saltpeter (potassium or sodium nitrate) soluable ingredients are carried off through a washing process; banks usually referred to a mound of earth used for safe storage of the finished product or other explosive materials.

Limestone — also called limerock, a fluxing agent used in the iron-making process to remove impurities, the by-product of which is slag. Limestone was formed by accumulation of organic remains such as shells.

Mantle — an annular ring on a blast furnace which supports the wall or shell and the brickwork of the inwall or shaft so that when necessary the firebrick lining of the combustion chamber can be removed without disturbing the inwall.

Moulders — ironworkers engaged in the activity of molding iron into predetermined shapes using either sand molds or metal cast boxes.

Nitre Works — a facility in which gunpowder or similar substances might be produced.

Pig iron — iron that has been run directly into "pigs" or sand molds from a blast furnace; cast iron.

Pneumatic process — See Bessemer Converter.

Q-BOP Furnace — a modern steel furnace utilizing a basic oxygen process and capable of producing large amounts of metal. A Q-BOP at U.S. Steel's Fairfield Works can produce more than 3600 tons a day.

Railroad iron — iron rolled into rails.

Red ore — hematite, iron ore type which replaced brown ore as the basis for the American iron industry, the iron content of which is the equivalent of 70%.

Rolling mill — a mill which rolls ingots into various shapes including slabs or finished products such as rails, beams or plates. Common in England in the early 1700s, rolling mills used rolls that were smooth-surfaced iron cylinders which pressed hot metal into thin flat sheets. In 1783 Henry Cort took out a patent for a mill with grooved rolls making it possible to roll iron into finished shapes.

Slag — the impurities and waste fluxing materials produced in liquid form in the making of iron in a blast furnace which substance separates from the iron consisting of sand, clay, ash, etc.

Smelter — an early name for an ironworks, an apparatus that extracts metal from ores by means of heating it to a high temperature in the presence of fluxing material such as limestone. The original iron smelter was a bowl-shaped hole in the ground lined with clay using animal skin bellows to aid in combustion; process improved upon by the Romans.

Steel — iron subjected to intense heat and mixed with carbon to give it added hardness and strength; also sometimes mixed with alloys.

Strap iron — an early name for iron rolled into rails or strap rails.

Wrought iron — a malleable iron put together from pasty particles low in carbon and not requiring fusion.

Glossary terms taken from the following source books:

J. M. Camp, C. B. Francis, The Making, Shaping and Treating of Steel, United States Steel Company, Pittsburgh, Pennsylvania, 1951.

Iron Age, Handbook of Terms Commonly Used in the Steel and Nonferrous Industries, Philadelphia, Pennsylvania, 1971.

Richard Moldenke, Library of Iron and Steel, Principles of Iron Founding, Vol. III, McGraw-Hill, New York, New York, 1917.

Ellsworth Newcomb, Hugh Kenny, Miracle Metals, G. P. Putnam's Sons, New York, New York, 1962.

Douglas Alan Fisher, The Epic of Steel, Harper & Row, Publishers, New York, New York, 1963.

MARKINGS FROM AN EARLIER DAY — Republic Iron and Steel Company marked its Tannehill property — this from the No. 2 Furnace rear mantle — with the lettering, R.I.S.CO. It acquired the property in 1899.

NOTES

CHAPTER I

[1] Rupert Hicks, *The Iron and Steel Industry in Alabama*, (Alabama Department of Industrial Relations, Montgomery, Ala., 1950), p. 2.

[2] Sir Charles Lyell, *A Second Visit to the United States of North America*, (John Murray, London, England, 1849), Vol. II, p. 81.

[3] Virginia Van Der Veer Hamilton, *Alabama, A History*, (W. W. Norton and Company, New York, New York, 1977), p. 12.

[4] Ethel Armes, *The Story of Iron and Coal in Alabama*, (1910 reprint ed., Book-keepers Press, Birmingham, Alabama, 1972), p. 52.

[5] Statistical Abstracts of the United States, Bulletins Nos. 12, 23, 44, 63, 81 and 100 (United States Printing Offices, Washington, D.C.).

[6] Characteristics of the Population/Alabama, Vol. 1, Part 2 (United States Department of Commerce, Washington, D.C., 1973), pp. 2-14.

[7] H. H. Chapman, *The Iron and Steel Industries of the South*, (University of Alabama Press, Tuscaloosa, Alabama, 1953), p. 99.

[8] Mary Gordon Duffee, *Sketches of Alabama: Being An Account Of The Journey From Tuscaloosa To Blount Springs Through Jefferson County On The Old Stage Roads* (University of Alabama Press, Tuscaloosa, Alabama, 1970), p. 5. (Edited by Virginia Pounds Brown and Jane Porter Nabors, this volume carries Miss Duffee's accounts as published in a series of 59 separate articles in the *Birmingham Weekly Iron Age* from 1885 to 1887.

[9] Armes, *Story of Coal and Iron in Alabama*, p. 52.

[10] Willis Brewer, *Alabama, Her History, Resources, War Record and Public Men* (The Reprint Publishing Company, Spartanburg, South Carolina, 1975; originally published 1872), pp. 81-82.

[11] Weymouth T. Jordan, *Ante-bellum Alabama, Town and Country* (Florida State University Press, Tallahassee, Florida, 1957), p. 146.

[12] Marjorie Longenecker White, *The Birmingham District, An Industrial History and Guide* (Birmingham Publishing Company, Birmingham, Alabama, 1981), pp. 36-37.

[13] Michael Tuomey, *Geology of Alabama, First Biennial Report* (M.D.J. Slade, Tuscaloosa, Alabama, 1850), p. 15.

[14] Armes, p. 68.

[15] Tuomey, *Geology of Alabama*, Preface x, xi.

[16] Charles G. Summersell, *Alabama, History for Schools* (American Southern, Northport, Alabama, third ed., 1965), p. 220.

[17] J. Frank Glazner, "The Importance of the Iron Industry in the Great Appalachian Valley of Alabama to the Confederacy" (*Southern Magazine*, August, 1934, Vol. 1, No. 5, News Publishing Company, Wytheville, Virginia), p. 22.

[18] Hicks, *The Iron and Steel Industry in Alabama*, p. 3.

CHAPTER II

[19] Joseph H. Woodward II, *Alabama Blast Furnaces* (Woodward Iron Company, Woodward, Alabama, 1940), p. 54.

[20] Bradford C. Colcord, *The History of Pig Iron Manufacture in Alabama* (American Iron and Steel Institute, Birmingham, Alabama, October 24, 1950), p. 1.

[21] Woodward, *Alabama Blast Furnaces*, p. 51.

[22] Armes, p. 96.

[23] Woodward, p. 53, 123, 126.

[24] Ibid.

[25] Ibid.

[26] Hamilton, *Alabama, A History*, p. 15.

[27] Woodward, p. 117, 74.

[28] Ibid.

[29] Armes, p. 183, 171.

[30] Ibid.

[31] Woodward, p. 105.

[32] James M. Swank, *The Manufacture of Iron in All Ages* (American Iron and Steel Association, Philadelphia, Pennsylvania, 1892), p. 230.

[33] Colcord, *History of Pig Iron Manufacture in Alabama*, p. 6.

[34] Woodward, p. 110.

[35] Chapman, *The Iron and Steel Industries of the South*, p. 100.

CHAPTER III

[36] Armes, p. 61.

[37] White, *The Birmingham District, An Industrial History and Guide,* p. 39.

[38] Duffee, *Sketches of Alabama,* p. 14.

[39] John Witherspoon DuBose, Jefferson County and Birmingham, Alabama (Temple & Smith Publishers, Birmingham, Alabama, 1887), p. 585.

[40] DuBose, Jefferson County and Birmingham, Alabama, p. 585.

[41] Armes, p. 61.

[42] Duffee, p. 14.

[43] Eastern Valley, Land Use Patterns and Development Pressures in Southwest Jefferson County, Office of Planning and Community Development, Jefferson County, Alabama, June, 1978, p. 3.

[44] Roupes Valley, Verticle Files, #684, Alabama Department of Archives and History, Montgomery, Alabama.

[45] Armes, p. 41, 62.

[46] Ibid.

[47] *Jones Valley Times,* April 15, 1851.

[48] James H. Walker, Jr., *Roupes Valley* (Montezuma Press, Bessemer, Alabama, 1972), p. 55.

[49] Josiah Gorgas Diary, Gorgas Papers, Special Collections, University of Alabama Library, University of Alabama, Tuscaloosa, Alabama, August 10, 1865.

[50] Woodward, p. 136.

[51] Ibid.

[52] Armes, p. 64.

[53] Leah Rawls Atkins, *The Valley and the Hills, An Illustrated History of Birmingham and Jefferson County* (Windsor Publications, Woodland Hills, California, 1981), p. 46.

[54] Armes, p. 64, 65.

[55] Ibid.

[56] Ibid.

[57] Ibid.

[58] Woodward, p. 117.

[59] Armes, p. 67.

[60] A. B. Moore, *History of Alabama and Her People* (The American Historical Society, Chicago, Illinois, 1927), pp. 410-411.

[61] Agricultural and Manufacturing Census, 1860, Bibb County, Alabama, microfilm, Birmingham Public Library, Birmingham, Alabama.

[02] *Modern Castings Magazine,* August, 1970, American Foundrymen's Society, Des Plaines, Illinois), p. 106.

[63] Agricultural and Manufacturing Census, 1850, Tuscaloosa County, Alabama, microfilm, Birmingham Public Library, Birmingham, Alabama.

[64] Chriss H. Doss, "A Paper of Historical Details About Oxmoor" (Furnace) given at the dedication of the Oxmoor Furnace Historical Marker, Alabama Historical Association, May 2, 1980, p. 2.

[65] Woodward, p. 138.

[66] Confederate States of America, The War Department, CSA Imprint, Communication of February 17, 1865 from Secretary of War John C. Breckinridge to Jefferson Davis, Special Collections, University of Alabama Library, University of Alabama, Tuscaloosa, Alabama. (The Confederate House of Representatives on December 24, 1864 requested a report on the number and location of Southern iron furnaces and forges under government contract, which information was transmitted to President Davis.)

[67] William T. Hogan, *Economic History of the Iron and Steel Industry in the United States* (D. C. Heath and Company, Lexington, Massachusetts, 1971), p. 28.

[68] Republic Steel Corporation memo, Rickey, Alabama, June 18, 1926 listing an inventory of the remaining old parts of the Tannehill Furnaces, Maxwell Papers, Special Collections, University of Alabama Library, University of Alabama, Tuscaloosa, Alabama.

[69] Confederate States of America, CSA Imprint, Breckinridge letter to Davis, p. 7.

70 Jim Hoffman, *Roupes Valley Ironworks and the Origin of Iron Production in Alabama,* 1829-1865, Masters thesis, University of Alabama, Tuscaloosa, Alabama, 1983, p. 89.

71 Frank E. Ardrey Jr., *Southern's Family History,* Southern Railroad Company, Montgomery, Alabama, 1960, p. 54. (This information was compiled from the *Legal History of Southern Railway Company* by Fairfax Harrison, Southern Railway Company Archives Department, Altanta, Georgia.)

72 Armes, p. 159.

73 *Modern Castings,* AFS Transactions, p. 105.

74 Confederate States of America, Breckinridge letter, pp. 8-9.

75 Clarence Sellers, interview, November 7, 1985. A Boy Scout leader in nearby Hueytown, Mr. Sellers was instrumental in the major clearing operation that led to opening Tannehill Historical State Park in 1970 by more than 300 scouts.

76 Letter from W. L. Sanders, owner of the Tannehill Ironworks, to the Shelby Iron Company, June 14, 1864, W. L. Chew Collection, Samford University Library, Samford University, Birmingham, Alabama.

77 Joseph H. Woodward II, "Alabama Iron Manufacturing," Alabama Review (Alabama Historical Association), July, 1954, p. 202.

78 Confederate Records, Breckinridge letter, p. 6.

79 Woodward, *Alabama Blast Furnaces,* p. 138.

80 Walter L. Fleming, *The Civil War and Reconstruction in Alabama* (Peter Smith, Gloucester, Massachusetts, 1949), p. 161. Originally published in 1905.

CHAPTER IV

81 William S. Hoole, Elizabeth H. McArthur, *The Yankee Invasion of West Alabama* (Confederate Publishing Company, Tuscaloosa, Alabama, 1985), p. 7.

82 Colcord, p. 6.

83 Robert H. McKenzie, "Reconstruction of the Alabama Iron Industry, 1865-1880," The Alabama Review (Alabama Historical Association), July, 1972, p. 179.

84 Colcord, p. 7.

85 Clement Eaton, *A History of the Southern Confederacy* (MacMillan Company, New York, 1954), pp. 135-136.

86 Victor S. Clark, *History of Manufacturers in the United States,* Vol. II, 1860-1893 (McGraw-Hill, New York, New York, 1929), p. 43.

87 Charles B. Dew, *Ironmaker to the Confederacy* (Yale University Press, New Haven, Connecticut, 1966), p. 143.

88 CSA Imprint. Letter from A. T. Jones, president of the Shelby Iron Company to Charles B. Mitchell, member of the Confederate Senate, April 26, 1864, Special Collections, University of Alabama Library, Tuscaloosa, Alabama, p. 5.

89 Letter from A. T. Jones to Sen. Charles B. Mitchell, p. 7.

90 Ralph E. Kirk, "Early History of the Most Essential Raw Materials for Manufacture of Iron and Steel in Alabama, 1798-1899," speech given to the Ensley Kiwanis Club, Birmingham, Alabama, January 23, 1958, Special Collections, University of Alabama Library, Tuscaloosa, Alabama, p. 9.

91 Milo B. Howard Jr., "Tannehill Furnace and the Confederacy," speech delivered during dedication ceremonies for the Confederate memorial at Tannehill Historical State Park, October 26, 1977. (Mr. Howard was director of the Alabama Department of Archives and History from 1967 to 1981.)

92 White, *The Birmingham District, An Industrial History,* p. 141.

93 Woodward (ABF), p. 23.

94 U.S. War Department, *The War of the Rebellion: A Compilation of the Official Records of the Union and Confederate Armies,* 129 vols. (Government Printing Office, Washington, D.C., 1880-1901), Series IV, Vol. III, pp. 832-833.

95 Confederate States of America, Breckinridge letter, p. 5.

96 Fleming, *Civil War and Reconstruction in Alabama,* p. 151.

97 Moore, *History of Alabama,* p. 550.

98 James Pickett Jones, *Yankee Blitzkrieg; Wilson's Raid Through Alabama and Georgia* (University of Georgia Press, Athens, Georgia, 1976), p. 86.

[99] Mrs. B. B. Ross, "The Selma Arsenal Memorial," *Southern Magazine,* News Publishing Company, Wytheville, Virginia, August, 1934, p. 21.

[100] *War of the Rebellion,* Series I, Vol. 49, p. 484.

[101] Armes, p. 194.

[102] *War of the Rebellion,* Series I, Vol. 49, Part I, p. 420.

[103] George Monlux, "To My Comrads of Company I,"/Private Papers, Iowa State Historical Department, Des Moines, Iowa, February 13, 1933. (A 136-page unpublished narrative of movements of Company I, Eighth Iowa Cavalry, during Wilson's Raid through Alabama during March and April, 1865. Contains an eyewitness report on the attack on the Tannehill Ironworks, March 31, 1865.)

[104] Letter from Addison S. Ruby, veteran of Company D, Eighth Iowa Cavalry, USA, to James A. Anderson, September 10, 1934, Anderson Papers, Special Collections, University of Alabama Library, University of Alabama, Tuscaloosa, Alabama.

[105] Monlux, "To My Comrads in Company I," 1933, p. 66.

[106] Theodore F. Rodenbough, *The Cavalry: The Photographic History of the Civil War* (Fairfax Press, New York, New York, 1983), p. 140.

[107] Armes, p. 187.

[108] Col. William H. Powell, *List of Officers of the Army of the United States* (L. R. Hamersly and Company, Detroit, Michigan, 1900), p. 616.

[109] Hoole and McArthur, *Yankee Invasion of West Alabama,* pp. 66-68.

CHAPTER V

[110] Josiah Gorgas Diary, Gorgas Collection, University of Alabama Library, Tuscaloosa, Alabama, p. 246.

[111] Gorgas Diary, p. 246

[112] Marty Everse, *The Iron Works at Brierfield: A History of Iron Making in Bibb County, Alabama* (unpublished manuscript, 1984), p. 31.

[113] Woodward (ABF), p. 139.

[114] Armes, p. 230.

[115] Woodward (ABF), p. 63, 142.

[116] Ibid.

[117] Daniel Augustus Tompkins Papers, William R. Perkins Library, Duke University, Durham, North Carolina, Letter from Mr. Tompkins to his fiancee, Miss Harriet Brigham, April 6, 1881. (Daniel Tompkins, who later became an important late - 19th Century industrialist in North Carolina, considered buying the old Tannehill Furnace site in 1881.)

[118] Armes, p. 334.

[119] Woodward (ABF), p. 43.

[120] Armes, p. 67.

CHAPTER VI

[121] Fleming, p. 155.

[122] White, p. 224.

[123] Colcord, p. 9.

[124] Hamilton, p. 128.

[125] Armes, p. 219, 221.

[126] Ibid.

[127] Hamilton, p. 128, 130, 131.

[128] Ibid.

[129] Ibid.

[130] Woodward (ABF), pp. 37-38.

[131] White, p. 46.

[132] Hamilton, p. 131.

[133] Janyth S. Tolson, Camilla G. Musgrove, Peter K. Sokolosky, Alabama Coal Data, Geological Survey of Alabama, University of Alabama, 1983, pp. 4-5.

[134] Swank, *Manufacture of Iron in All Ages,* p. 231.

135 Everett Smith, Randall S. Epperson, *Minerals in Alabama, Geological Survey of Alabama*, Information Series 64-B, University of Alabama, 1984, p. 22.

136 Hicks, p. 2.

137 Ibid.

138 A. V. Wiebel, *Biography of a Business* (Tennessee Coal and Iron Division, United States Steel Corporation, Birmingham, Alabama, 1960), p. 24.

139 Armes, p. 290.

140 Wiebel, *Biography of a Business*, p. 22.

141 Thomas McAdory Owen, *History of Alabama and Dictionary of Alabama Biography*, Vol. III (Reprint Company, Spartanburg, South Carolina, 1978), p. 815. (Originally published in 1921)

142 Wiebel, p. 24.

143 Hamilton, p. 132.

144 Wiebel, p. 30.

145 Hamilton, p. 136.

146 Armes, P. 353, 356, 299.

147 Ibid.

148 Ibid.

149 Woodward (ABF), pp. 156-158.

150 Armes, p. 301, 358.

151 Ibid.

152 *A Little Journey in the Birmingham District*, American Chemical Society, Spring Meeting, April 3-7, 1922, Birmingham, Alabama (booklet), p. 13-14.

153 Alabama State Employment Service Reports, 1945, 1953, 1960, 1970, 1980, 1983 (Alabama Department of Industrial Relations, Montgomery, Alabama.)

CHAPTER VII

154 Armes, pp. 160-161.

155 Sellers Interview, November 7, 1985.

156 U. K. Roberts, interview, May 22, 1985. Retired from U.S. Steel, Mr. Roberts is known as the historian of Tannehill Historical State Park and regularly gives tours of the furnace area.

157 Republic Steel Corporation memo, June 18, 1926.

158 Letter from H. D. Whitson, clerk, Board of Revenue, Tuscaloosa County to Fred Maxwell, consulting engineer, University of Alabama, July 20, 1951, Maxwell Papers, Special Collections, University of Alabama Library, Tuscaloosa.

159 David L. DeJarnette, Thomas H. DeJarnette, Jr., *Archaeological Investigation of the Tannehill Blast Furnaces* (Alabama Museum of Natural History, University of Alabama, Tuscaloosa, 1956), foreword.

160 DeJarnette, *Archaeological Investigation of the Tannehill Blast Furnaces*, foreword.

161 DeJarnette, p. 9, 29.

162 Letter from Fred R. Maxwell, Jr., consulting engineer for the University of Alabama, to Earl McGowin, Director, State Department of Conservation and Natural Resources, July 6, 1951 (Maxwell Papers, Special Collections, University of Alabama Library, Tuscaloosa.)

163 Alabama Act No. 994, Regular Session, 1969 (SB 748 - Skidmore, Gilmore, Morrow, Vacca, Bailes, Hawkins, Dominick, Givhan, McCarley, Childs, passed September 12, 1969, p. 1.

164 Agricultural and Manufacturing Census, 1870, Jefferson County, Alabama, microfilm, Birmingham Public Library, Birmingham, Alabama.

165 Walker, *Roupes Valley*, pp. 99-100.

166 *Old Tannehill* (American Revolution Bicentennial Administration/Institutional Development and Economic Affairs Service, Washington, D.C., 1976), p. 25. A technical report on the re-firing of Tannehill No. 1 111 years after becoming an industrial casualty of the Civil War.

[167] *Fire in the Furnace* (U.S. Steel Corporation, Southern Steel Division, Birmingham, Alabama, 1977), p. 5. This booklet was compiled and researched by the Office of Public Affairs at Birmingham-Southern College in cooperation with the Tannehill Furnace and Foundry Commission.

[168] *Tuscaloosa News,* Tuscaloosa, Alabama, September 20, 1976.

[169] Letter from Walter B. Jones, state geologist to Fred R. Maxwell, Jr., consulting engineer, University of Alabama, December 4, 1952 (Maxwell Papers, Special Collections, University of Alabama Library, Tuscaloosa.)

[170] Hobart M. Kraner, "Ceramics in the Saugus Blast Furnace, Circa 1650" (Ceramic Bulletin, American Ceramic Society, Chicago, Illinois, Vol. 39, No. 7, 1960), p. 355.

[171] *Modern Castings Magazine,* AFS Transactions, August, 1970, p. 105.

[172] *Old Tannehill,* p. 12.

[173] Atkins, *The Valley and the Hills,* p. 46.

EPILOGUE

[174] McKenzie, "Reconstruction of the Alabama Iron Industry, 1865-1880," p. 179.

[175] Woodward, "Alabama Iron Manufacturing, 1860-1865,'" p. 207.

[176] Census of Manufactures, 1963, Alabama-SIC 3312, Bureau of the Census, U.S. Department of Commerce, Washington, D.C.

[177] Colcord, p. 10; Woodward (ABF), p. 37

[178] Colcord, pp. 12-13, p. 16; *A Little Journey in the Birmingham District,* American Chemical Society, p. 19.

BIBLIOGRAPHY

Most of the books and references included in this bibliography are available in the larger libraries of Alabama, the University of Alabama Library in Tuscaloosa or the State Department of Archives and History in Montgomery. An excellent review of the 81 iron furnaces built in Alabama from 1815 to 1940 can be found in *Alabama Blast Furnaces* published by Woodward Iron Company in 1940.

Ardrey, Frank E., Jr., *Southern's Family History*, Southern Railway Company, Montgomery, Alabama, 1960.

Armes, Ethel. *The Story of Coal and Iron in Alabama*, Book-keepers Press, Birmingham, Alabama, 1972 reprint; originally published 1910.

Atkins, Leah Rawls. *The Valley and the Hills, An Illustrated History of Birmingham and Jefferson County*, Windsor Publications, Woodland Hills, California, 1981.

Brewer, Willis. *Alabama, Her History, Resources, War Record and Public Men*, Re-print Publishing Company, Spartanburg, South Carolina, 1975; originally published 1872.

Chapman, H. H. *The Iron and Steel Industries of the South*, University of Alabama Press, Tuscaloosa, Alabama, 1953.

Clark, Victor S. *History of Manufacturers in the United States*, Vol. II, 1860-1893, McGraw-Hill, New York, New York, 1929.

Colcord, Bradford C. *The History of Pig Iron Manufacture in Alabama*, American Iron and Steel Institute, Birmingham, Alabama, October 24, 1950.

DeJarnette, David L. and Thomas H., Jr. *Archaeological Investigation of the Tannehill Blast Furnaces*, Museum of Natural History, University of Alabama, Tuscaloosa, 1956.

Dew, Charles B. *Ironmaker to the Confederacy*, Yale University Press, New Haven, Connecticut, 1966.

Doss, Chriss H. "A Paper of Historical Details About Oxmoor (Furnace)" given at the dedication of the Oxmoor Furnace Historical Marker, Alabama Historical Association, May 2, 1980.

DuBose, John Witherspoon. *Jefferson County and Birmingham, Alabama, Historical and Biographical, 1887*, Temple & Smith, Publishers, Birmingham, Alabama, 1887.

Duffee, Mary Gordon. *Sketches of Alabama: Being An Account Of The Journey From Tuscaloosa to Blount Springs Through Jefferson County On The Old Stage Roads*, University of Alabama Press, Tuscaloosa, 1970; originally published in a series of 59 articles appearing in the *Birmingham Weekly Iron Age* from 1885 to 1887.

Eaton, Clement. *A History of the Southern Confederacy*, MacMillan Company, New York, New York, 1954.

Everse, Martin L. *The Iron Works at Brierfield, A History of Ironmaking in Bibb County, Alabama,* unpublished manuscript, 1984.

Fleming, Walter L. *The Civil War and Reconstruction in Alabama,* Peter Smith, Gloucester, Massachusetts, 1949.

Fire in the Furnace, A Technical Report on the Refiring of Tannehill Furnace No. 1, 111 Years After Becoming an Industrial Casualty of the Civil War, United States Steel Corporation, Office of Public Affairs, Birmingham-Southern College, 1977.

Glazner, J. Frank. "The Importance of the Iron Industry in the Great Appalachian Valley to the Confederacy," *Southern Magazine,* Vol. 1, No. 5, August, 1934.

Gorgas, Josiah, Diary. University of Alabama Library, Special Collections, Tuscaloosa, 1865.

Hamilton, Virginia Van Der Veer. *Alabama, A History,* W. W. Norton and Company, New York, New York, 1977.

Hicks, Rupert. *The Iron and Steel Industry in Alabama,* Alabama Department of Industrial Relations, Montgomery, 1950.

Hoffman, Jim. *Roupes Valley Ironworks and the Origin of Iron Production in Alabama,* 1829-1865, Masters thesis, University of Alabama, Tuscaloosa, 1983.

Hogan, William T. *Economic History of the Iron and Steel Industry in the United States,* D. C. Heath and Company, Lexington, Massachusetts, 1971.

Hoole, William S., McArthur, Elizabeth H. *The Yankee Invasion of West Alabama,* Confederate Publishing Company, Tuscaloosa, Alabama, 1985.

Howard, Milo B. "Tannehill Furnace and the Confederacy," remarks delivered during dedication of the United Daughters of the Confederacy Memorial, Tannehill Historical State Park, October 26, 1977.

Jones, James Pickett. *Yankee Blitzkreig; Wilson's Raid Through Alabama and Georgia,* University of Georgia Press, Athens, 1976.

Jones Valley Times, Elyton, Alabama, April 15, 1851.

Jordan, Weymouth T. *Ante-bellum Alabama, Town and Country,* Florida State University Press, Tallahassee, 1957.

Kirk, Ralph E. "Early History (1798-1899) of the Most Essential Raw Materials for Manufacture of Iron and Steel in Alabama," speech given to the Ensley Kiwanis Club, Birmingham, Alabama, January 23, 1958 (Special Collections, University of Alabama Library, Tuscaloosa, Alabama).

Kraner, Hobart M. "Ceramics in the Saugus Blast Furnace, Circa 1650," Ceramic Bulletin, American Ceramic Society, Chicago, Illinois, Vol. 39, No. 7, 1960.

Little Journey in the Birmingham District, American Chemical Society, Spring Meeting booklet, April 3-7, 1922, Birmingham, Alabama.

Lyell, Sir Charles. *A Second Visit to the United States of North America,* John Murray, London, England, Vol. II, 1849.

McKenzie, Robert H. "Reconstruction of the Alabama Iron Industry, 1865-1880," The Alabama Review, Alabama Historical Association, Tuscaloosa, July, 1972.

Modern Castings, American Foundrymen's Society, AFS Transactions, Des Plaines, Illinois, August, 1970.

Monlux, George. "To My Comrads of Company I," Private Papers, Iowa State Historical Department, Des Moines, 1933.

Moore, A. B. *History of Alabama and Her People,* The American Historical Society, Chicago, Illinois, 1927.

Owen, Thomas McAdory. *History of Alabama and Dictionary of Alabama Biography,* Vol. III, Reprint Company, Spartanburg, South Carolina, 1978 (1921).

Powell, Col. William H. List of Officers of the Army of the United States, L. R. Hamersly and Company, Detroit, Michigan, 1900.

Republic Steel Corporation, memo from Rickey Mine on iron artifacts at the nearby Tannehill Furnace site, June 18, 1926 (Maxwell Papers, University of Alabama Library, Tuscaloosa).

Rodenbough, Theodore F. *The Cavalry, The Photographic History of the Civil War,* Fairfax Press, New York, New York, 1983.

Ross, Mrs. B. B. "The Selma Arsenal Memorial," *Southern Magazine,* News Publishing Company, Wytheville, Virginia, August, 1934.

Swank, James M. *The Manufacture of Iron in All Ages,* American Iron and Steel Association, Philadelphia, Pennsylvania, 1892.

Summersell, Charles G. Alabama, *History for Schools,* American Southern, Northport, Alabama, 1965.

Tuomey, Michael, *Geology of Alabama, First Biennial Report,* M.D.J. Slade, Tuscaloosa, Alabama, 1850.

Tuscaloosa News, Tuscaloosa, Alabama, September 20, 1976.

U.S. War Department, TheWar of the Rebellion: A Compilation of the Official Records of the Union and Confederate Armies, Government Printing Office, Washington, D.C., 1880-1901.

Walker, James H., Jr. *Roupes Valley, A History of the Pioneer Settlement of Roupes Valley Which is Located in Tuscaloosa and Jefferson Counties, Alabama,* Montezuma Press, Bessemer, Alabama, 1972.

White, Marjorie Longenecker. *The Birmingham District, An Industrial History and Guide,* Birmingham Publishing Company, Birmingham, Alabama, 1981.

Wiebel, A. V. *Biography of a Business,* Tennessee Coal and Iron Division, United States Steel Corporation, Birmingham, Alabama, 1960.

Woodward, Joseph H., II. *Alabama Blast Furnaces,* Woodward Iron Company, Woodward, Alabama, 1940.

Woodward, Joseph H., II, "Alabama Iron Manufacturing," Alabama Review, Alabama Historical Association, Tuscaloosa, Alabama, July, 1954.

OTHER GOVERNMENT DOCUMENTS

Alabama Acts, Act No. 994, Regular Session, 1969, passed as SB 748 . . . creating the Tannehill Furnace and Foundry Commission as a state agency.

Alabama Coal Data, Geological Survey of Alabama, Janyth S. Tolson, Camilla G. Musgrove, Peter K. Sokolosky, University of Alabama, Tuscaloosa, 1983.

Alabama State Employment Service Reports, 1945, 1953, 1960, 1970, 1980, 1983, Alabama Department of Industrial Relations, Montgomery.

Agricultural and Manufacturing Census, 1850, Tuscaloosa County, Alabama (Birmingham Public Library).

Agricultural and Manufacturing Census, 1860, Bibb County, Alabama (Birmingham Public Library).

Agricultural and Manufacturing Census, 1870, Jefferson County, Alabama (Birmingham Public Library).

Census of Manufactures, 1963, Alabama-SIC 3312, Bureau of the Census, U.S. Department of Commerce, Washington, D.C.

Characteristics of the Population/Alabama, Vol. 1, Part II, United States Department of Commerce, Washington, D.C., 1973.

Eastern Valley, Land Use Patterns and Development Pressures in Southwest Jefferson County, Office of Planning and Community Development, Jefferson County, Alabama, June, 1978.

Minerals in Alabama, Geological Survey of Alabama, Information Series 64-B, Everett Smith, Randall S. Epperson, University of Alabama, Tuscaloosa, 1984.

Statistical Abstracts of the United States, Bulletins Nos. 12, 23, 44, 63, 81 and 100, Government Printing Office, Washington, D.C.

LETTERS, INTERVIEWS

Confederate States of America, The War Department, CSA Imprint, Communication of February 17, 1865 from Secretary of War John C. Breckinridge to Jefferson Davis, President of the Confederacy (University of Alabama Library).

Letter from Fred R. Maxwell, consulting engineer for the University of Alabama, to Earl McGowin, Director, State Department of Conservation and Natural Resources, Montgomery, July 6, 1951 (University of Alabama Library, Maxwell Papers).

Letter from H. D. Whitson, clerk, Tuscaloosa County, to Fred R. Maxwell, consulting engineer, University of Alabama, July 20, 1951 (Maxwell Papers, University of Alabama Library).

Letter from Walter B. Jones, state geologist, to Fred R. Maxwell, consulting engineer, University of Alabama, December 4, 1952 (University of Alabama, Maxwell Papers).

Interview with U. K. Roberts, Tannehill Historical State Park historian, May 22, 1985.

Letter from Addison S. Ruby, veteran of Company D, Eighth Iowa Cavalry, USA to James A. Anderson, September 10, 1934 (Anderson Papers, University of Alabama Library).

Letter from W. L. Sanders, owner of the Tannehill Ironworks, to the superintendent of the Shelby Ironworks, June 14, 1864 (Chew Papers, Samford University Library, Birmingham, Alabama).

Letter from Daniel Augustus Tompkins, prospective Tannehill Furnace buyer, to his fiancee, Miss Harriet Brigham, April 6, 1881 (Tompkins Papers, Duke University Library, Durham, North Carolina).

Letter from A. T. Jones, president of the Shelby Iron Company to Hon. Charles B. Mitchell, member of the Confederate Senate, April 26, 1864 (Special Collections, CSA Imprint, University of Alabama Library, Tuscaloosa, Alabama).

Interview with Clarence Sellers, Scout Master, Boy Scout Troop 207, Hueytown, Alabama, November 7, 1985.

Letter from E. R. Riddle to Samuel S. Riddle, Holidaysburg, Huntingdon County, Pennsylvania, July 28, 1842 (Private Papers, Heritage Hall, Talladega Heritage Commission, Talladega, Alabama).

Letter from Dr. Frank A. Rose, President of the University of Alabama to Ed Lewis, lieutenant governor, Alabama Central District, Civitan International, April 26, 1967. (Iron and Steel Museum of Alabama).

ACKNOWLEDGEMENTS

In the forward march of human progress man, it seems, all too often neglects to look over his shoulder at where he's been. The road to the present is marked by significant milestones, the proper reading of which can give insight into what lies ahead.

To be sure, Alabama is unfamiliar ground to out-of-state tourists. Many Alabamians themselves know far too little about their state's founding families, its pioneer industries and its colorful history.

This book is an effort to open the doorway a bit into the state's industrial past and to closely examine what happened 150 years ago at a placed called Old Tannehill, the first iron plant in the Birmingham district.

Certainly no work of this scope can be written without extensive research. Ours has taken us from private papers tucked away in homes of old Alabama families to the archives of the State Historical Society of Iowa. The unfolding of Tannehill's history at times seemed to be taking place with a nod from the Creator himself. Valuable materials, much of it never before published, ended up in the writer's office, some sought after, some just sent by mail.

To the many persons who contributed, in ways both large and small, I offer my sincere appreciation.

I am especially indebted to the members of the Tannehill Furnace and Foundry Commission who urged me to undertake this project and to Dean Margaret Sizemore Douglass, Chriss H. Doss, A. B. Schwarzkopf, Ed Nelson and J. Morgan Smith who reviewed this work and offered editorial suggestions.

I also offer my grateful appreciation to the following, who in their private or official capacities, rendered great assistance: Elizabeth Wells, Special Collections librarian, Samford University Library, Birmingham; Joyce Lamont, curator, Special Collections, University of Alabama Library, Tuscaloosa; Dr. Leah Rawls Atkins, director of the Arts and Humanities Center, Auburn University; Malcolm M. MacDonald, director of the University of Alabama Press, Tuscaloosa and Donnell L. Ruthenberg, library associate, State Historical Society of Iowa, Des Moines.

Appreciation is also extended to Dr. Marvin Whiting, archivist, Birmingham Public Library and Jeannie Scott, former head of the Library's Southern History Department; Edwin C. Bridges, director, Alabama Department of Archives and History, Montgomery; Annette Watters, assistant director, Center for Business and Economic Research, University of Alabama, Tuscaloosa; Robert E. Weller, state programs administrator, State Department of Industrial Relations, Montgomery and Lewis E. McCray, executive director, West Alabama Planning and Development Council, Tuscaloosa.

A special word of thanks is given further to John Baker, resident vice president, Norfolk Southern Railroad, Montgomery; Ray L. Farabee, retired professor of metallurgy, University of Alabama, Tuscaloosa; Sloan Hill, director, public affairs, U.S. Steel Corporation, South, Birmingham; Vicki

Gentry, director, Iron and Steel Museum of Alabama, Tannehill Historical State Park and Marty Everse, executive director, Brierfield Ironworks Park, Brierfield, Alabama.

Others rendering valuable assistance included Bates Wilson and Martin Christie, U.S. Pipe and Foundry Company; Bob Palmer, Gene Hollis, Tildon Drake and J. B. White, LTV Steel Corporation; P. R. Satterwhite, Mead Land Services and Bob Brantley, State Employment Service, Birmingham.

Thanks also go to Ann Marshall of Tuscaloosa, who researched the Confederate contract with the Tannehill Ironworks; Pat Bray, editor of the *Shades Valley Sun*, who proofed the manuscript; and to David Glenn, Clarence Sellers and James Walker, whose advice proved very helpful in pulling together loose pieces of history.

In addition to the many rare photographs used in this volume provided by the State Department of Archives and History, the Iron and Steel Museum of Alabama, Samford University, the Birmingham Public Library and U.S. Steel Corporation, George Flemming and Joe Aloia, III went beyond all expectations in providing modern-day shots of Tannehill Historical State Park.

In putting together such a list as this, one always runs the risk of omitting someone who has also made a contribution. Certainly no such omission was intended. To all those who helped please accept my heartfelt thanks.

JRB

INDEX

The past is but the beginning of the beginning, and all that is said and has been is but the twilight of the dawn.

— H. G. Wells